# Worksheets Don't Grow Dendrites

## Third Edition

# Worksheets Don't Grow Dendrites

Third Edition

*20 Instructional Strategies*
*That Engage the Brain*

**Marcia L. Tate**

CORWIN
A SAGE Company

FOR INFORMATION:

Corwin

A SAGE Company

2455 Teller Road

Thousand Oaks, California 91320

(800) 233-9936

www.corwin.com

SAGE Publications Ltd.

1 Oliver's Yard

55 City Road

London EC1Y 1SP

United Kingdom

SAGE Publications India Pvt. Ltd.

B 1/I 1 Mohan Cooperative Industrial Area

Mathura Road, New Delhi 110 044

India

SAGE Publications Asia-Pacific Pte. Ltd.

3 Church Street

#10-04 Samsung Hub

Singapore 049483

Acquisitions Editor:  Jessica Allan

Senior Associate Editor:  Kimberly Greenberg

Editorial Assistant:  Katie Crilley

Production Editor:  Veronica Stapleton Hooper

Copy Editor:  Terri Lee Paulsen

Typesetter:  C&M Digitals (P) Ltd.

Proofreader:  Dennis W. Webb

Indexer:  Marilyn Augst

Cover Designer:  Gail Buschman

Marketing Manager:  Stephanie Trkay

Copyright © 2016 by Corwin

Printed in the United States of America

*Library of Congress Cataloging-in-Publication Data*

Tate, Marcia L.
Worksheets don't grow dendrites : 20 instructional strategies that engage the brain / Marcia L. Tate. — Third edition

pages cm

Includes bibliographical references and index.

ISBN 978-1-5063-0273-7 (pbk. : alk. paper)

1. Effective teaching—Handbooks, manuals, etc. 2. Lesson planning—Handbooks, manuals, etc. 3. Learning. I. Title.

LB1025.3.T29 2016
371.102--dc23        2015028522

This book is printed on acid-free paper.

SFI  Certified Sourcing
www.sfiprogram.org
SFI-00453

17 18 19 10 9 8 7 6 5 4 3

# Contents

Acknowledgments                                                              ix

About the Author                                                              x

Introduction                                                                  1

Strategy 1:    Brainstorming and Discussion                                  15

What: Defining the Strategy                                                  15
Why: Theoretical Framework                                                  16
How: Instructional Activities                                                17
Reflection and Application                                                   22

Strategy 2:    Drawing and Artwork                                           25

What: Defining the Strategy                                                  25
Why: Theoretical Framework                                                  26
How: Instructional Activities                                                26
Reflection and Application                                                   30

Strategy 3:    Field Trips                                                   33

What: Defining the Strategy                                                  33
Why: Theoretical Framework                                                  34
How: Instructional Activities                                                34
Reflection and Application                                                   37

Strategy 4:    Games                                                         39

What: Defining the Strategy                                                  39
Why: Theoretical Framework                                                  40
How: Instructional Activities                                                41
Reflection and Application                                                   47

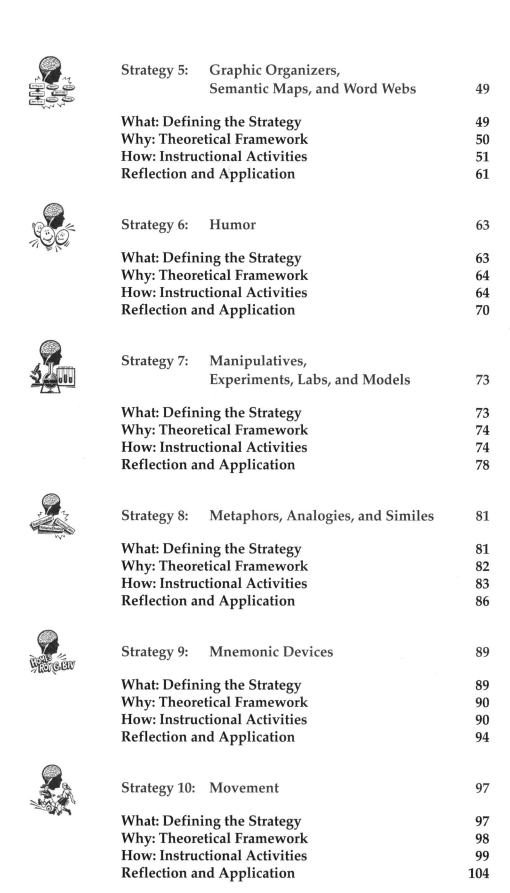

Strategy 5:   Graphic Organizers,
              Semantic Maps, and Word Webs          49

What: Defining the Strategy                         49
Why: Theoretical Framework                          50
How: Instructional Activities                       51
Reflection and Application                          61


Strategy 6:   Humor                                 63

What: Defining the Strategy                         63
Why: Theoretical Framework                          64
How: Instructional Activities                       64
Reflection and Application                          70


Strategy 7:   Manipulatives,
              Experiments, Labs, and Models         73

What: Defining the Strategy                         73
Why: Theoretical Framework                          74
How: Instructional Activities                       74
Reflection and Application                          78


Strategy 8:   Metaphors, Analogies, and Similes     81

What: Defining the Strategy                         81
Why: Theoretical Framework                          82
How: Instructional Activities                       83
Reflection and Application                          86


Strategy 9:   Mnemonic Devices                      89

What: Defining the Strategy                         89
Why: Theoretical Framework                          90
How: Instructional Activities                       90
Reflection and Application                          94


Strategy 10:  Movement                              97

What: Defining the Strategy                         97
Why: Theoretical Framework                          98
How: Instructional Activities                       99
Reflection and Application                          104

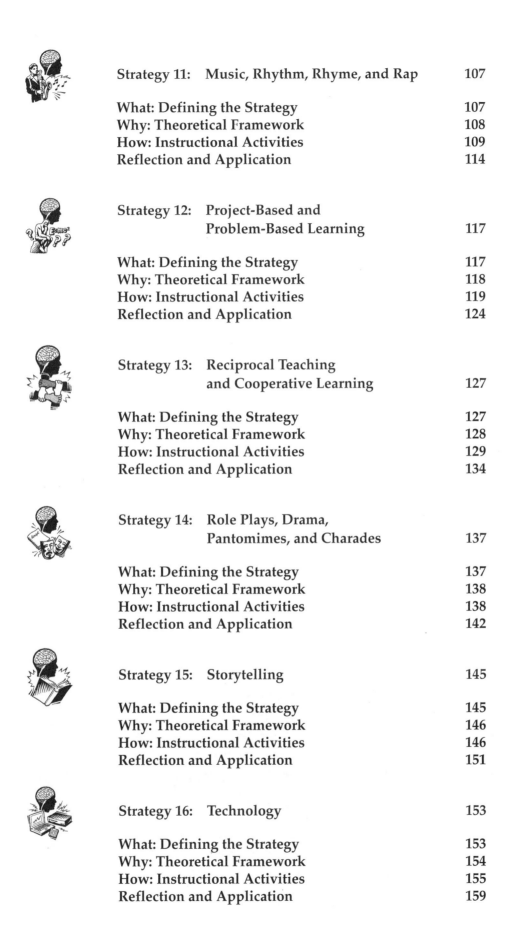

**Strategy 11:   Music, Rhythm, Rhyme, and Rap**          107

What: Defining the Strategy          107
Why: Theoretical Framework          108
How: Instructional Activities          109
Reflection and Application          114


**Strategy 12:   Project-Based and
                Problem-Based Learning**          117

What: Defining the Strategy          117
Why: Theoretical Framework          118
How: Instructional Activities          119
Reflection and Application          124


**Strategy 13:   Reciprocal Teaching
                and Cooperative Learning**          127

What: Defining the Strategy          127
Why: Theoretical Framework          128
How: Instructional Activities          129
Reflection and Application          134


**Strategy 14:   Role Plays, Drama,
                Pantomimes, and Charades**          137

What: Defining the Strategy          137
Why: Theoretical Framework          138
How: Instructional Activities          138
Reflection and Application          142


**Strategy 15:   Storytelling**          145

What: Defining the Strategy          145
Why: Theoretical Framework          146
How: Instructional Activities          146
Reflection and Application          151


**Strategy 16:   Technology**          153

What: Defining the Strategy          153
Why: Theoretical Framework          154
How: Instructional Activities          155
Reflection and Application          159

**Strategy 17:   Visualization and Guided Imagery**          161

    **What: Defining the Strategy**          161
    **Why: Theoretical Framework**          162
    **How: Instructional Activities**          163
    **Reflection and Application**          166

**Strategy 18:   Visuals**          169

    **What: Defining the Strategy**          169
    **Why: Theoretical Framework**          170
    **How: Instructional Activities**          171
    **Reflection and Application**          174

**Strategy 19:   Work Study and Apprenticeships**          177

    **What: Defining the Strategy**          177
    **Why: Theoretical Framework**          178
    **How: Instructional Activities**          179
    **Reflection and Application**          182

**Strategy 20:   Writing and Journals**          185

    **What: Defining the Strategy**          185
    **Why: Theoretical Framework**          186
    **How: Instructional Activities**          187
    **Reflection and Application**          191

**Resource A:   Brain-Compatible Lesson Plan**          193

**Resource B:   Graphic Organizers**          205

**Bibliography**          219

**Index**          225

# Acknowledgments

It is my belief that every student comes to school with an inherent gift, a package, so to speak. It is the educator's job to unwrap this gift by finding the most viable means through which each student can excel. As society has changed, so has the packaging, necessitating the need for a variety of ways of unwrapping these packages.

My gratitude goes to those educational consultants who are giving us additional ways to unwrap these gifts by translating the findings of the neuroscientists into educational practice and to those teachers who use interactive strategies daily to engage the brains of their students.

Speaking of gifts, I am deeply grateful for family members and professional educators who have supported me through and assisted me with the writing of my seven bestsellers. To my husband of over 35 years and best friend, Tyrone, whose steadfast belief and constant encouragement enable me to unwrap each day with enthusiasm and a belief that all things are possible.

To my dearest children—Jennifer, Jessica, and Christopher, I write this book for them as much as anyone since their learning styles are as different as their personalities. Teachers could unwrap Jenny's gifts by involving her in hands-on activities. Jessie could always adapt her gifts to the instruction provided. Chris, on the other hand, needed to be bodily engaged in the task at hand. He had to draw, build, and move to be successful. Unless his teachers used these strategies, school was a struggle for my son and many times, his gifts were not unwrapped. I dedicate this book to them, to my five beautiful grandchildren, and to the numerous parents in my workshops who have told me that their children learn similarly to mine.

To the associates who present for our company, Developing Minds Inc., thank you for using your gifts to help us spread the word. To our administrative assistants, Carol Purviance and Fran Rodrigues, your gifts of organization and technical expertise enable us to enhance our gifts. Working with all of you to improve instruction daily for every student is truly a present.

# About the Author

**Marcia L. Tate** is the former executive director of professional development for the DeKalb County Schools in Decatur, Georgia. During her 30-year career with the district, she has been a classroom teacher, reading specialist, language arts coordinator, and staff development executive director. Marcia was named Staff Developer of the Year for the state of Georgia, and her department was selected to receive the Exemplary Program award for the state.

Marcia is currently an educational consultant and has presented her workshops to over 450,000 administrators, teachers, parents, and community leaders from all over the United States and the world, including Australia, Canada, Egypt, Hungary, Oman, New Zealand, Singapore, and Thailand. She is the author of the following seven bestsellers: *Worksheets Don't Grow Dendrites: 20 Instructional Strategies That Engage the Brain* (2nd ed.); *"Sit & Get" Won't Grow Dendrites: 20 Professional Learning Strategies That Engage the Adult Brain* (2nd ed.); *Reading and Language Arts Worksheets Don't Grow Dendrites: 20 Literacy Strategies That Engage the Brain* (2nd ed.); *Mathematics Worksheets Don't Grow Dendrites: 20 Numeracy Strategies That Engage the Brain; Science Worksheets Don't Grow Dendrites: 20 Instructional Strategies that Engage the Brain; Shouting Won't Grow Dendrites: 20 Techniques to Detour Around the Danger Zones* (2nd ed.); and *Preparing Children for Success in School and Life: 20 Ways to Increase Your Child's Brain Power.* She is also the author of *Social Studies Worksheets Don't Grow Dendrites: 20 Instructional Strategies that Engage the Brain.* Marcia has written a number of published articles and chapters that have been included in other books. Participants in her workshops call them some of the best ones they have ever attended since Marcia models the 20 strategies in her books to actively engage her audiences.

She received her bachelor's degree in psychology and elementary education from Spelman College in Atlanta, her master's in remedial reading from the University of Michigan in Ann Arbor, and her specialist and doctorate degrees in educational leadership from Georgia State University and Clark Atlanta University, respectively. Spelman College awarded her the Apple Award for excellence in the field of education.

Marcia is married to Tyrone Tate and is the proud mother of three children, Jennifer, Jessica, and Christopher. If she had known how wonderful it would be to be a grandmother, Marcia would have had her five grandchildren, Christian, Aidan, Maxwell, Aaron, and Roman, before she had her children. She and her husband own the company Developing Minds, Inc. and can be contacted by calling the company at (770) 918–5039, by e-mailing her at marciata@bellsouth.net, or by visiting her website at www.developingmindsinc.com.

# Introduction

## SCENARIO I

Dr. Tyler teaches English II at Lakewood High School. The bell rings for class to begin but students are still engaged in conversation in the hall. Dr. Tyler moves to the door and strongly encourages students to go to their seats. Some comply immediately. Others do not. The roll is checked and the lesson begins.

The objective of today's lesson is to teach students to make inferences about the structure and elements of drama. The source of the drama happens to be Scene 3 from Sophocles's *Antigone.* Dr. Tyler conducts a quick review of Scenes 1 and 2, where he lectures students on the most important events in the play while students listen and take notes.

During the next part of the lesson, Dr. Tyler calls on various students to read aloud the parts of Creon and Haemon, the two main characters in Scene 3, while the remainder of the class follows along in their textbooks (which, by the way, weigh about 10 pounds each). Dr. Tyler never establishes a purpose for the reading so students never really know what they are to focus on as they listen while the play is being read aloud. After about a 25-minute period, students are given 15 additional minutes to read the remainder of Scene 3 silently. Some are reading with interested faces. Others have their heads on their desks while one young lady in the back of the room has her cell phone inside her English book and is secretly texting.

Students are then provided a sheet containing 10 inference questions that need to be answered in writing. These include the following:

- *What is Creon's view of a good son?*

- *What is Creon's view of women?*

- *How does the tone of the dialogue between Creon and Haemon change from the beginning to the end of the scene?*

Two minutes prior to the ringing of the bell, students are instructed to turn in the answers to the questions and prepare for dismissal. They are reminded that tomorrow's lesson will focus on Scene 4 of *Antigone* and in order to be prepared for the subsequent discussion, students should read that scene for homework.

## SCENARIO II

The second scenario can be told from a first-person perspective since it describes a lesson that I actually taught to a group of English II students in Mesquite, Texas. With classical music playing softly in the background, I stood at the door as students were changing classes so that I could shake the hand of every high school student as he or she entered class. I introduced myself as their teacher for the period and noticed that there were some students who did not know which hand to extend or how to look me in the eye and say *Good afternoon!* Therefore, before I began the lesson that I was asked to teach, I taught the interpersonal skills necessary for one person to greet another. Many of these students were either already working or would be seeking jobs in the near future and needed to be able to appropriately introduce themselves to their prospective employers.

I had been asked by the instructor to teach Scene 3 of Sophocles's *Antigone.* I hooked students into the lesson by talking about the genre of drama and comparing the drama in this play to the drama in the television reality series of *The Real Housewives of Atlanta* (especially since I am from Atlanta). I also reminded them that housewives in Atlanta are actually nothing like those portrayed in the reality show. After all, I am a housewife of Atlanta. They laughed!

Each student selected a close partner and, as a review, I asked them to take turns retelling the major events in Scenes 1 and 2 of the play to their partner. I then conducted a whole class discussion where students reviewed the salient events from both scenes. I told students that by the time this lesson is finished, they will be able to make inferences regarding the structure and elements of *Antigone* and cite text evidence to support their understanding.

Four different duos of students volunteered to assume the roles of Creon and Haemon and came to the front of the room to stand and read those parts. I told them that they would need to read with fluency and expression since we did not need to be bored right after lunch! I really think that one student tried to outdo another in their ability to read dramatically as if they were the actual character. The remainder of the class constituted the Choragos, a chorus of the elders of Thebes, and stood each time the chorus spoke to read aloud in a choral response.

I divided Scene 3 into chunks and gave students some probing inferential questions to think about prior to reading each chunk, such as the ones mentioned in Scenario 1. In a spirited discussion, during which I called on volunteers and nonvolunteers, students had to show evidence from the text that supported the inferences they made regarding Creon's viewpoints. This discussion gave me some idea of how well they were accomplishing the objective. I also provided them with additional inference questions to discuss with their partners prior to writing down the answers. The time flew by and soon the period was over.

You know you have taught a memorable lesson when you tell students that time is up and many of the students respond, *Awwww!* On the way out of the room, a student stopped to tell me that this lesson was one of the best ones she had experienced the entire school year! This comment made all of the planning and execution worthwhile. By the way, I did not have a single behavior problem during the entire period!

In two high school English II classes the same content is being taught, but teachers are using different methodology. The difference in instructional practices makes a huge difference! I am not crediting the success of my lesson to my superior ability as a teacher. I am crediting it to the brain-compatible instructional strategies used in the lesson and described in detail in the chapters which follow.

# BRAIN-COMPATIBLE INSTRUCTION

*One learns to do by doing.*

—Aristotle

*Tell me, I forget.*

*Show me, I remember.*

*Involve me, I understand!*

—Old Chinese Proverb

Thousands of years of history support one major concept. When students are actively engaged in experiences with content, they stand a much better chance of learning and remembering what we want them to know. Yet with increased emphasis on *high-stakes testing*, teachers are apt to spend the majority of time using worksheets and lecture to teach lower-level concepts that can be best assessed by paper and pencil.

Learning-style theorists (Gardner, 1983; Marzano, 2007; Sternberg & Grigorenko, 2000) and educational consultants (Jensen, 2008, 2009b; Sousa, 2011; Willis, 2006, 2007a) have concluded that there are some instructional strategies that, by their very nature, result in long-term retention. Those strategies are addressed in numerous books about the brain but were not previously delineated in any one text. Now they are!

For more than 20 years, I have been studying the awesome functions of brain cells. Through my extensive reading, participation in workshops and courses with experts on the topic, and my observations of best practices in classrooms throughout the world, I have synthesized these instructional strategies into 20 methods for delivering instruction. And those strategies work for the three following reasons:

1. They increase academic achievement for *all* of the following students: students who are in elementary, middle, high school, and college; students who are in gifted classes, regular education classes, and special education classes; students for whom English is a second language; and students who are learning across the curriculum.

2. They decrease behavior problems by minimizing the boredom factor in class and increasing the confidence factor in those students who would use their inadequacy as a cause for misbehavior.

3. They make teaching and learning fun for all grade levels so that even students taking calculus are just as excited about learning as the kindergarten student on the first day of school.

The 20 strategies are as follows:

1. Brainstorming and discussion

2. Drawing and artwork

3. Field trips

4. Games

5. Graphic organizers, semantic maps, and word webs

6. Humor

7. Manipulatives, experiments, labs, and models

8. Metaphors, analogies, and similes

9. Mnemonic devices

10. Movement

11. Music, rhythm, rhyme, and rap

12. Project-based and problem-based learning

13. Reciprocal teaching and cooperative learning

14. Role plays, drama, pantomimes, and charades

15. Storytelling

16. Technology

17. Visualization and guided imagery

18. Visuals

19. Work-study and apprenticeships

20. Writing and journals

As millions of dollars are being spent in an effort to find cures for brain abnormalities such as Alzheimer's disease, dementia, and Parkinson's disease, more and more information is being gleaned about the brain. Teachers should be the first to avail themselves of this information since they are teaching the brains of students each and every day. In fact, I tell teachers that the next time they complete a résumé, they need to include that they are not only *teachers but also gardeners*—better known as *dendrite growers*—because every time students learn something new in their classrooms, they grow a new brain cell, called a dendrite.

Refer to Figure 0.1 for a correlation of these 20 strategies to Howard Gardner's Theory of Multiple Intelligences as well as to the four major learning modalities: (1) visual, (2) auditory, (3) kinesthetic, and (4) tactile. Each lesson that incorporates multiple modalities not only increases students' test scores but also stands a better chance of being remembered by students long after the teacher-made, criterion-referenced, or standardized tests are over. After all, isn't that why we teach—long-term retention?

The book you are about to read attempts to accomplish five major objectives:

1. Delineate the characteristics of a classroom that takes advantage of the way student brains' learn best;

2. Review the research regarding the 20 brain-compatible strategies, as well as best practices in instruction regardless of the content area;

3. Supply more than 200 examples of the application of the 20 strategies for teaching objectives at a variety of grade levels and in multiple cross-curricular areas;

4. Provide time and space at the end of each chapter for the reader to reflect on the application of the strategies as they apply directly to the reader's specific objectives; and

5. Demonstrate how to plan and deliver unforgettable lessons by asking the five questions on the lesson plan format contained in the Resource section of the book.

The brain-compatible activities in each chapter are only samples of lessons that can be created when the strategies are incorporated from kindergarten to calculus. They are intended only to get the reader's brain cells going, as they think up a multitude of additional ways to deliver effective instruction to their students.

When you really examine the list of 20, you will find that they are used most frequently in the primary grades. It is when the strategies begin to disappear from the repertoire of teachers that students' academic achievement, confidence, and love for school also diminish. You may remember the book, *Everything I Needed to Know I Learned in Kindergarten*. This also applies to teaching. If every teacher would teach the way a kindergarten teacher teaches, most students would learn. The content should change, but the way of delivering that content should not.

What if every teacher used the 20 strategies, including art, drama, music, and storytelling, to teach the academic subject areas of English, mathematics, science and social studies? Would we not see more students graduating at the end of high school? After all, *If students don't learn the way we teach them, then we must teach them the way they learn.* Here's an analogy. When you go fishing, do you use bait you like or bait the fish likes? There are 20 instructional strategies that brain research shows that your students will like and that you should be using as bait.

This book is the foundational text in a series of multiple, cross-curricular bestsellers about *growing dendrites*. The books are as follows:

- *Worksheets Don't Grow Dendrites: 20 Instructional Strategies That Engage the Brain*, **Second Edition**
- *"Sit & Get" Won't Grow Dendrites: 20 Professional Learning Strategies That Engage the Adult Brain*, **Second Edition**
- *Reading and Language Arts Worksheets Don't Grow Dendrites: 20 Literacy Strategies That Engage the Brain*, **Second Edition**
- *Shouting Won't Grow Dendrites: 20 Techniques to Detour Around the Danger Zones*, **Second Edition**

- *Mathematics Worksheets Don't Grow Dendrites: 20 Numeracy Strategies That Engage the Brain, PreK–8*
- *Science Worksheets Don't Grow Dendrites: 20 Instructional Strategies That Engage the Brain*
- *Social Studies Worksheets Don't Grow Dendrites: 20 Instructional Strategies That Engage the Brain*

The activities outlined in each chapter of this text are designed to be starting points for planning lessons that are intended to be brain compatible and are in no way meant to be an exhaustive list of possibilities. The advantage of having activities that range from elementary through high school in the same book is that the reader can easily select activities that will meet the needs of students performing below, on, and above grade level and can, therefore, more easily differentiate instruction. You will also find that an activity designated for a specific grade range can be taken as is or easily adapted to fit the grade level that the reader is teaching. Therefore, as you peruse this text, examine not only those activities in each content area that are age or grade appropriate but also look for ones at other grade levels that can easily meet your needs once you change the conceptual level of the material.

The reflection page at the end of each chapter enables readers to reflect on the activities that they are already using that incorporate the strategy and to add others to their repertoire. The lesson planning section helps the reader synthesize the process of planning unforgettable lessons by asking and answering the five essential questions on the plan.

## Characteristics of a Brain-Compatible Environment

Teachers who use the brain-compatible instructional strategies addressed in the chapters which follow for lesson design and delivery deserve to have a classroom environment that is likewise, brain compatible. Teachers who are not able to create these environments for their students have students who may not be excelling at optimal levels. My observations in hundreds of classrooms and knowledge of brain-compatible instruction tell me that there are 10 characteristics of classrooms where students tend to excel. After you peruse the 10, your project will be to identify those characteristics that you are already very comfortable implementing and to identify two that you will work on for the next 21 days. Why 21 days? That is how long it will take to make those two characteristics a habit in your daily instruction. You see, I have a theory. No matter how wonderful you are, you should be making specific plans to become even better!

### (1) A Positive Environment

When you enter a brain-compatible classroom, you know it immediately! The teacher is standing at the door smiling and greeting students, asking them about their weekends or evenings, and complimenting them on some positive aspect of their lives. Did you know that the word *SMILE* is a mnemonic device which stands for *Show Me I'm Loved Everyday!* Students are not loitering in the hall but are entering class, excited about what they can expect in the day's lesson. As the class proceeds, there is an obvious air of enthusiasm and optimism in the room. The teacher loves his or her subject matter, and students are supporting each other in the learning and not putting one another down, as I see in so many classrooms. Students are confident that they can be successful and know that if a concept is not understood that the teacher and peers are there to assist and support. Consult Strategy 4: "Games" and Strategy 6: "Humor" for specific activities that will help you create a positive environment.

## (2) Visuals

We live in a very visual world! With computers, video games, smartphones, television, and the like, students' brains are absorbing a great deal of information visually. At least 50% of students who walk into any classroom today will be predominately visual learners. Another 35% will be kinesthetic, which is why they need to be moving, but we will discuss that under another characteristic. This means that if your primary method for delivering instruction is auditory, then *Houston, We Have a Problem!* Only 15% of the class is listening. Brain-compatible teachers accompany their lectures with images from the SMART board or document camera, video clips, virtual field trips, and so forth. They even ensure that those visuals on the wall in the peripheral vision of students are content related.

Teachers often worry about having to take down visuals from the walls prior to a test. I tell teachers, *Do not dismay!* If those visuals have been up long enough, even if you remove them, your students can still visualize what was on the wall. Consult Strategy 17: "Visualization and Guided Imagery" and Strategy 18: "Visuals" for specific ways to engage the visual modalities of students.

## (3) Music

As students are assembling, brain-compatible teachers have soft, calming music playing and students have learned from day one that if the teacher hears their voices over the music, they are talking too loudly! This music is used around 30% of the time but never while the teacher is delivering direct instruction. It can be distracting to many students to have music playing while your expectation is that students are giving you their undivided attention.

So when do these teachers play music? It may be when students are working together in cooperative groups, writing creatively, or solving math problems. The type of music used during these times should probably be instrumental with no lyrics, and the volume should be turned extremely low so as not to disturb the thought processes of students. At other times, these teachers want high-energy, motivational music that can be interwoven with the content or played during transition times or during an engaging activity. Consult Strategy 11: "Music, Rhythm, Rhyme, and Rap" for specific activities for infusing music into your classroom.

*(4) Relevant Lessons*

What came first—school or brains? Of course, human beings had brains long before there was a formal place called school. Therefore, the purpose of the brain was never to make straight *A*s or score high on a standardized or teacher-made test. The purpose of the brain is survival in the real world. Wouldn't it make sense then, that those things in real life that are crucial to man's survival are more easily remembered than those that are needed for tests in school?

I know that at some point in your teaching career, a student has asked you this question, *Why do we have to learn this?* When students cannot see the connection between what is being taught in school and their personal lives, they will often ask the question. Brain-compatible teachers attempt to take the objective they are teaching and relate it to students' personal lives. For example, rather than using the math problems in the book initially, these teachers create real-life problems and integrate the students' names into the problems so that they can actually see themselves solving them.

*(5) Rituals Taught*

A brain-compatible classroom is an active, engaging classroom but never a chaotic classroom. It is the teacher's routines, expectations, and procedures that have been determined, taught, and practiced so often that they have become rituals that keep the classroom orderly and organized. In fact, effective classroom managers spend more time teaching those rituals than teaching their content at the beginning of the school year or term. When done well, this enables the teacher to spend more time teaching the content for the remainder of the year.

Students have to know how you expect them to begin and end class, when to talk and when to be quiet and listen, when to move and when to remain in their seats, or how to get into groups when cooperative learning is warranted. Chapter 14: "Teach Your Rituals" in the bestseller *Shouting Won't Grow Dendrites: 20 Techniques to Detour Around the Danger Zones* (2nd ed.) gives definitive suggestions for teaching and practicing those determined routines, expectations, and procedures.

*(6) Students Talking About Content*

The person doing the most talking about the content is growing the most dendrites, or brain cells, regarding the content. In many classrooms I observe in that is the teacher. In a brain-compatible classroom, it should be the students. Making all students a part of the conversation helps to ensure that the content is understood and remembered. The teacher's job comes prior to the lesson—that of planning a lesson that can then be facilitated when it is taught. Some teachers have very unrealistic expectations—that students will sit quietly for long periods of time and are even chastised for wanting to converse with their friends. Yet, we learn 70% to 90% of what we are capable of teaching to someone else. Strategy 1: "Brainstorming and Discussion" and Strategy 13: "Reciprocal Teaching and Cooperative Learning" will provide teachers with multiple ways in which to engage the brains of students as they process information.

### (7) Students Moving to Learn Content

Students sit entirely too much! Brain-compatible teachers have students moving at certain points during the lesson knowing that this behavior will give them some relief from sitting on the most uncomfortable piece of furniture known to man, the student desk. More importantly, movement correlates to long-term retention. Anything that one learns while moving is hard-wired into one of the strongest memory systems in the brain. If you have ever driven a stick shift, you will never forget how to do it—even if you have been driving an automatic for years. A football coach in Texas once made the comment in a workshop that this research explains why football players who may not remember the content in class can remember every play on the field. Movement is probably my favorite strategy since it not only correlates with long-term retention, it also makes teaching and learning so much fun! Consult Strategy 10: "Movement" and Strategy 14: "Role Plays, Dramas, Pantomimes, and Charades" for additional research to support the need to have students in motion.

### (8) High Expectations

More than 50 years of research, beginning at Harvard University in the 1960s with the work of Dr. Robert Rosenthal and his famous 1968 study, *Pygmalion in the Classroom* with Lenore Jacobson, point to the fact that one gets what one expects. If teachers don't expect much from their students, they will not get much from those students. If the expectations are high and teachers give students the confidence to believe that they can meet those expectations, then exceptional things can happen. Instilling confidence in students should be a major part of the equation. A sports figure with the confidence to do well in a game has a much better chance of doing well than one who doesn't have such confidence. When the confidence in a game shifts from one team to another, that concept is known as a *momentum shift* and can often determine the outcome of the game. We all have seen instances where one sports team was not as skilled as another and yet beat the more skilled team simply because they believed they could.

Brain-compatible teachers visualize every student in their class being successful! If a teacher cannot see that success, it is not likely to happen. One teacher related to me that on the first day of class each year, she has every student write the word *can't* on a piece of paper. Then she has students symbolically shred the paper and throw it in the trash. She then, teaches students this motto: *Success comes in cans, not in can'ts.*

## *(9) High Challenge, Low Stress*

A brain-compatible classroom is one where students are being consistently challenged but the stress level is low. There is no sense of accomplishment when people are successfully completing tasks that are too easy for them. If you don't believe that students want to be challenged, you have never watched them engage with video games that they have a difficult time abandoning. The creators of video games are smart and know how the brain reacts. Teachers would be wise to pay attention. Game makers have students start playing the game at an easy level where they can build up their confidence with appropriate responses. Then as soon as the student is hooked, the difficulty level of the game increases. Students continue to play because they have the continued confidence that they can move to a more difficult level and still be successful. In addition, no image has ever appeared on a video game that pops up with the following message, *You have failed! Stop playing!* Students can continue perfecting their craft until they get it right. Then they move on to the next, more difficult level. Brain-compatible classrooms are ones where students are consistently challenged but the probability of failure is low.

## *(10) Content Taught in Chunks With Activity*

It may surprise you to know that even the adult brain can hold an average of only seven isolated bits of information simultaneously. This is why so much in the world comes in a series of seven. This concept will be addressed in more detail in the lesson planning section of this book. Effective teachers teach in small parts or chunks. They know that the brain can only hold a limited amount of information at one time so they divide their lessons up into meaningful bites or chunks and feed students one chunk at a time until the entire lesson is digested.

Here's a story to illustrate my point. I attended the wedding of one of my daughter's friends when the minister did not chunk the wedding vows appropriately. The bride and groom were expected to repeat the vows after the minister. However, the minister gave the bride too much to say in the first chunk. I turned to my husband and commented that unless the bride had memorized her vows, she would never be able to remember all that she was given. Sure enough, when it was time for the bride to repeat the vows, she turned to the minister and asked, *Could you repeat that, please? I didn't get it all!* I really needed to give that minister some chunking lessons! Brain-compatible teachers divide the lesson into small parts and ensure that an activity is integrated into each part so that the brain has time to process the information contained in the chunk.

These are the 10 characteristics of a classroom that facilitates brain-compatible instruction. How many of them are already natural parts of your classroom? Which two will you work on for the next 21 days?

The remainder of this book centers on delivering brain-compatible lessons within that context. Turn the page and begin your journey down a path that may help to revolutionize your instructional practices or that may support the effectiveness of some of the practices that you are currently using.

**"How come the History Channel is so interesting and my history class is so boring?"**

SOURCE: Bacall (2003a).

**Table 0.1** Comparison of Brain-Compatible Instructional Strategies to Learning Theory

| Brain-Compatible Strategies | Multiple Intelligences | Visual, Auditory, Kinesthetic, Tactile (VAKT) |
|---|---|---|
| Brainstorming and discussion | Verbal-linguistic | Auditory |
| Drawing and artwork | Spatial | Kinesthetic/tactile |
| Field trips | Naturalist | Kinesthetic/tactile |
| Games | Interpersonal | Kinesthetic/tactile |
| Graphic organizers, semantic maps, and word webs | Logical-mathematical/ spatial | Visual/tactile |
| Humor | Verbal-linguistic | Auditory |
| Manipulatives, experiments, labs, and models | Logical-mathematical | Tactile |

| Brain-Compatible Strategies | Multiple Intelligences | Visual, Auditory, Kinesthetic, Tactile (VAKT) |
|---|---|---|
| Metaphors, analogies, and similes | Spatial | Visual/auditory |
| Mnemonic devices | Musical-rhythmic | Visual/auditory |
| Movement | Bodily-kinesthetic | Kinesthetic |
| Music, rhythm, rhyme, and rap | Musical-rhythmic | Auditory |
| Project-based and problem-based learning | Logical-mathematical | Visual/tactile |
| Reciprocal teaching and cooperative learning | Verbal-linguistic | Auditory |
| Role plays and drama, pantomimes, charades | Bodily-kinesthetic | Kinesthetic |
| Storytelling | Verbal-linguistic | Auditory |
| Technology | Spatial | Visual/tactile |
| Visualization and guided imagery | Spatial | Visual |
| Visuals | Spatial | Visual |
| Work study and apprenticeships | Interpersonal | Kinesthetic |
| Writing and journals | Intrapersonal | Visual/tactile |

# Strategy 1

## Brainstorming and Discussion

### WHAT: DEFINING THE STRATEGY

*The answer is 216. What is the question?*

*What is the author's purpose? Cite text evidence.*

*Discuss the design of an experiment that would test your hypothesis.*

*Are we controlling technology or is technology controlling us?*

*Do you agree with her answer? Why or why not?*

Participants in my workshops can be some of the chattiest people in the world. This fact is based on my more than 25 years of teaching teachers and administrators. Yet, some of those same people who love to and should talk to one another in my classes, will not let their students participate in that same behavior in their own classrooms. Many students get in trouble for doing something that comes so naturally to the human brain—talking.

When people open their mouths to speak, they send more oxygen to the brain. If the brain is deprived of oxygen for three or more minutes, it can be declared dead. I have observed in some classrooms where students are breathing but it is hard to tell. Just visualize the scene from the movie, *Ferris Bueller's Day Off* where the teacher, Ben Stein, is asking *Anyone? Anyone?* and the high school students are figuratively brain dead. I show that scene in my workshops.

Another benefit of talking facilitates the growth of dendrites. Having students discuss the answers to open-ended questions, express opinions, or brainstorm a variety of ideas is advantageous to the brain. According to Allen and Currie (2012), during discussion, students *can increase the amount of paper manipulated and stored into the filing cabinets of the brain, slowly forming a more complex outlook on the topic* (p. 41).

# WHY: THEORETICAL FRAMEWORK

When students talk and share ideas, it is more likely that they will process the information and remember what they have learned (Sousa & Pilecki, 2013).

Reading assignments that are preceded with background information and followed by discussion enable students to gain more from the assignment (Marsh, 2013).

When students are engaged in collaborative conversations during formative assessment, those discussions can support many of the Common Core State Standards, such as speaking and listening (McLaughlin & Overturf, 2013).

Having students dialogue with peers who have different perspectives is a civic engagement strategy used in social studies to help students prepare for becoming competent and responsible citizens (National Council for the Social Studies, 2010).

When students talk about a topic, they will understand it better because their brains not only mentally process the information but they verbally process it as well (Allen, 2008).

Brainstorming or group discussion activities, in cooperation with graphic organizers, encourage all students to contribute (Jensen, 2007).

The quality and quantity of the questions that real-life scientists ask determines the progress of science in the real world (Berman, 2008).

Students up to the age of 10 learn better when an academic discussion is directed by the teacher. Adolescents and adults benefit from discussions led by a cooperative group (Jensen, 2007).

When a new math skill is viewed within the context of a problem, English language learners have opportunities to develop language skills through discussion (Coggins, Kravin, Coates, & Carrol, 2007).

The most widely known technique for stimulating creativity in the brain is probably the act of brainstorming where all ideas are accepted and there is a greater chance of reaching a workable solution (Gregory & Parry, 2006).

Students with special needs benefit when the class works in groups of fewer than six and the teacher uses directed response questioning so that students have a chance to think aloud (Jensen, 2007).

Teachers can guide students through very difficult solutions to mathematics problems by using a series of well-thought-out questions that address process rather than procedure (Posamentier & Jaye, 2006).

# HOW: INSTRUCTIONAL ACTIVITIES

**WHO:**                Elementary/Middle/High
**WHEN:**           Before a lesson
**CONTENT AREA(S):**    Cross-curricular

- Stauffer's (1975) Directed Reading Thinking Activity (DR-TA) has stood the test of time with both narrative and informational texts. Have students predict from a picture, a story title, or a chapter what the text will be about. Have them read a segment of text to confirm those predictions. Then have them make another prediction from the new text read. The sequence of predicting, validating, and predicting again continues until the end of the passage or text (Tate, 2014a, p. 23).

**WHO:**                Elementary/Middle/High
**WHEN:**           During a lesson
**CONTENT AREA(S):**    Cross-curricular

- Give students a content-area question to which there is more than one appropriate answer. Students brainstorm as many ideas as possible in a designated time while complying with the following *DOVE* guidelines:

  - *Defer* judgment when other students are contributing ideas.
  - *One* idea at a time is presented.
  - A *Variety* of ideas are encouraged.
  - *Energy* is directed to the task at hand.

**WHO:**                Elementary/Middle/High
**WHEN:**           During a lesson
**CONTENT AREA(S):**    Cross-curricular

- Use the process of close reading described below to help students comprehend complex texts. These steps can be implemented with the whole class and may take more than one or two days to complete.

  - Following little or no pre-reading discussion, introduce the text to students.
  - *First Reading*—Have students read the entire text by themselves without assistance.
  - *Second Reading*—Provide a fluent model by reading the entire text aloud. Stop periodically to discuss vocabulary, the historical or social context of the passage, or a complicated sentence structure. Do not explain the characters, ideas, or specific events in the text. Have students discuss the text.
  - Formulate questions that students can only answer from the text and pose them to the class. Students should not be able to rely on personal experiences to answer the questions.
  - *Third Reading*—Have students read the text and locate evidence to answer the text-dependent questions.

- When appropriate, have students use other brain-compatible strategies, such as music, art, role play, or graphic organizers, to improve comprehension of the text. Subsequent chapters of this book will address these strategies.
- Have students develop one concise sentence to answer each of the text-dependent questions.
- Have students provide orally or in writing an analysis of the text, including text-based evidence to support their analysis (McLaughlin & Overturf, 2013).

| | |
|---|---|
| **WHO:** | Elementary/Middle/High |
| **WHEN:** | During a lesson |
| **CONTENT AREA(S):** | Cross-curricular |

- When writing quality questions that can be used during discussion, Walsh & Sattes (2005) delineate the following five criteria for assessing those questions:

  - There should be a purpose in asking the question.
  - Each question should be clearly focused on the content.
  - Each question should engage students at multiple cognitive levels.
  - Each question should be concise and clear.
  - No question should be asked merely by chance.

| | |
|---|---|
| **WHO:** | Elementary/Middle/High |
| **WHEN:** | During or after a lesson |
| **CONTENT AREA(S):** | Cross-curricular |

- When asking questions in class or creating teacher-made tests, provide opportunities for all students to be successful by asking both knowledge or short-answer questions as well as those that enable students to use their reasoning, critical-thinking, and creative-thinking skills. Refer to the circles in Figure 1.1 to ensure that students have opportunities to answer questions at all levels of the revised Bloom's taxonomy, particularly those above the *Remembering* level.

| | |
|---|---|
| **WHO:** | Elementary/Middle/High |
| **WHEN:** | During or after a lesson |
| **CONTENT AREA(S):** | Cross-curricular |

- A different taxonomy is the *SOLO* pyramid in Figure 1.2. *SOLO* is a mnemonic device for *Structure of Observed Learning Outcomes* since it encourages students to think about where they are currently performing with their learning and what they need to do in order to make progress. The five main stages are as follows:

  - **Pre-structural**—*I am not sure about . . .*
  - **Uni-structural**—*I have one relevant idea about . . .*
  - **Multi-structural**—*I have several ideas about . . .*

- o **Relational**—*I have several ideas about . . .* or *I can link them to the big picture . . .*
- o **Extended Abstract**—*I have several ideas about . . . , I can link them to the big picture* and *I can look at these ideas in a new and different way.*

| | |
|---|---|
| **WHO:** | Elementary/Middle/High |
| **WHEN:** | During or after a lesson |
| **CONTENT AREA(S):** | Cross-curricular |

- During cooperative group discussions or as students create original questions for content-area assessments following a unit of study, have them use the verbs in Figure 1.1. These verbs will help to ensure that questions are created that represent various levels of thought.

| | |
|---|---|
| **WHO:** | Elementary/Middle/High |
| **WHEN:** | During or after a lesson |
| **CONTENT AREA(S):** | Cross-curricular |

- According to Bellanca, Fogarty, and Pete (2012), there are seven rigorous proficiencies in the area of thinking that students need to master. Each of the proficiencies has three explicit-thinking skills that can be taught from kindergarten through Grade 12 and across all curricular areas. They are as follows:

  - o **Critical Thinking**—Analyze, Evaluate, Problem Solve
  - o **Creative Thinking**—Generate, Associate, Hypothesize
  - o **Complex Thinking**—Clarify, Interpret, Determine
  - o **Comprehensive Thinking**—Understand, Infer, Compare
  - o **Collaborative Thinking**—Explain, Develop, Decide
  - o **Communicative Thinking**—Reason, Connect, Represent
  - o **Cognitive Transfer of Thinking**—Synthesize, Generalize, Apply

| | |
|---|---|
| **WHO:** | Elementary/Middle/High |
| **WHEN:** | During a lesson |
| **CONTENT AREA(S):** | Cross-curricular |

- Have students work with peers in *families* of four to six. During the lesson, stop periodically and have families discuss answers to questions related to what is being taught. For example, in math class, students could compare their answers to the homework assignment, and when answers differ, they could engage in a discussion to reach consensus as to the correct answer. Have students stay together with their families long enough to build relationships and then change the composition of the families.

| | |
|---|---|
| **WHO:** | Elementary/Middle/High |
| **WHEN:** | During a lesson |
| **CONTENT AREA(S):** | Cross-curricular |

- During discussions, sentence starters similar to the ones listed here are particularly effective for English language learners because they enable all students to take an active part:

    ○ I realize that . . .
    ○ I agree with _____ that _____.
    ○ I would like to add to _____'s idea.
    ○ I don't understand what _____ meant when she said _____. (Coggins et al., 2007)

**WHO:**                   Elementary/Middle/High
**WHEN:**                  During a lesson
**CONTENT AREA(S):**       Cross-curricular

- Use the **think, pair, share** technique with students. Pose a question or discussion topic to the class. Have them *think* of an individual answer. Then have them *pair* with a peer and *share* their answer. Then call on both volunteers and non-volunteers to respond to the entire class.

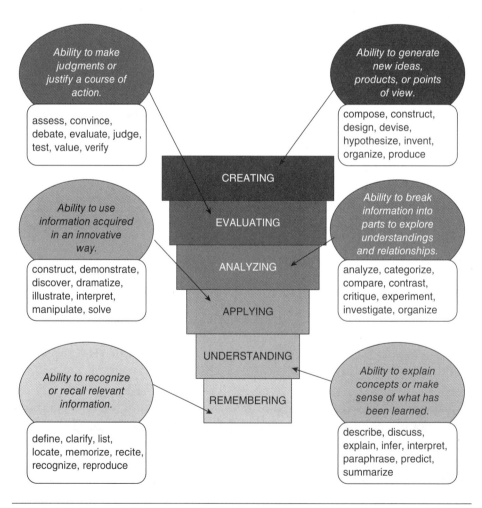

**Figure 1.1**   Bloom's Taxonomy (Revised)

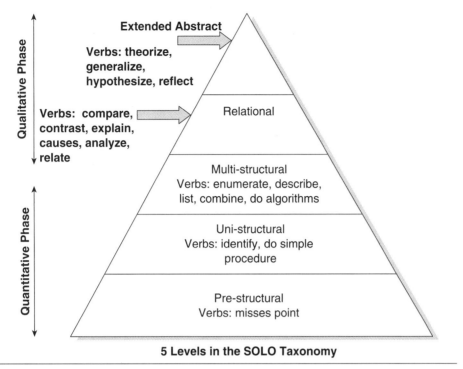

**Figure 1.2**   SOLO Taxonomy

SOURCE: John B. Biggs & K. Collis. Retrieved from www.educatingmatters.wordpress.com.

**WHO:**                          Elementary/Middle/High
**WHEN:**                         During a lesson
**CONTENT AREA(S):**              Cross-curricular

 • Present a controversial issue to the class, such as, *Are we controlling technology or is technology controlling us?* Divide the class in half and have them research and prepare a debate for one side of the issue or another. Then, actually role-play the debate by having students take turns serving on opposing teams and orally presenting their arguments to the class. You can be the judge of which side was more convincing at the culmination of the debate.

## REFLECTION AND APPLICATION

> **How will I incorporate *brainstorming and discussion* into instruction to engage students' brains?**

**Which brainstorming and discussion activities am I already integrating as I teach the curriculum?**

**What additional activities will I integrate?**

# Strategy 2

# Drawing and Artwork

## WHAT: DEFINING THE STRATEGY

I worked for 30 years with a major school district in the metropolitan Atlanta area. Even though I have been retired from that system since 2003, I still have a vested interest in the district. I have a granddaughter who goes to school in the district and a son-in-law who teaches physical education there. I was very concerned when I looked at the headlines of a neighborhood newspaper that arrived at my house. The cover story stated that 1,964 students, or one-fifth of the 2012 graduating class, would not be graduating. The article further stated that only two schools, a college academy and a school for the performing arts, graduated all of the students in the senior class. We know why the college academy students graduated. These students were already taking college courses. But why would the school of the performing arts graduate every student—not only in 2012, but in other years as well?

Could it be that these teachers are teaching to both hemispheres of the brain? Could it be that they are using drawing, music, and drama to teach the language arts, mathematics, science, and social studies? Could it be that if every teacher taught to both hemispheres of the brain, might we not see more students walk across the stage at graduation and receive their diplomas?

A person's ability to draw and design serves them well in the real world. Artists, architects, and interior designers are all paid well to use their unique abilities to transform the visual-spatial world around them. Yet in traditional classrooms, these talents are often perceived as interfering with instruction. I have seen students engaged in off-task behavior drawing imaginative cars, tennis shoes, superheroes, or celebrities of far greater interest than the boring lesson being taught in the front of the room.

For more than 70 years, researchers (Dewey, 1934; Fraser, 2013; Prystay, 2004) have written about the positive relationship between thinking in art and thinking across the curriculum. Yet when school budgets become tight, the art program is one of the first thought to be expendable. Educators need to think again!

## WHY: THEORETICAL FRAMEWORK

Art is key to the development of the human brain in children and continues to keep our minds sharp as we age (PBS, 2014).

The visual imagery children acquire when drawing is crucial for helping them to understand other curricular subjects such as math and geography (Fraser, 2013).

Putting ideas on paper through diagrams and sketches helps external memory and lessens the burden experienced when problem solving or remembering ideas (Busche, 2013).

Having students draw, paint, or use technology to create symbolic pictures that represent the knowledge they are learning is one way to help them store and manipulate information (Dean, Hubbell, Pitler, & Stone, 2012).

Drawing a nonlinguistic representation or image during instruction is a literacy strategy that can enable students to understand written sources (National Council for the Social Studies, 2010).

The success of the mathematician and scientist is because of skills taken from the tools of the artist such as accurate observation, spatial thinking, and kinesthetic perception (Sousa, 2006).

Having students add drawings or doodles to their notes helps them comprehend and encode new content for later recall (Allen, 2008).

When useful, teachers should encourage students to draw pictures in mathematics, which can help them gain more insight by representing abstract concepts graphically (Posamentier & Jaye, 2006).

"If a picture is worth a thousand words, perhaps drawing and visualizing can help science students enhance their learning potential" (National Science Teachers Association [NSTA], 2006, p. 20).

Math books in Singapore teach students to draw models in an effort to visualize math problems prior to solving them (Prystay, 2004).

Different areas of the brain, including the amygdala and the thalamus, are activated when people are involved in art activities (Jensen, 2001).

## HOW: INSTRUCTIONAL ACTIVITIES

**WHO:**                  Elementary/Middle/High
**WHEN:**                 During or after a lesson
**CONTENT AREA(S):**      Cross-curricular

• Give students an opportunity to create a personal *pictionary* by illustrating assigned content-area vocabulary words. Each page of the pictionary consists of an assigned word written in color, a drawing that depicts the meaning of the word, and an original sentence using the word in the appropriate context.

**WHO:**               Elementary/Middle/High
**WHEN:**              After a lesson
**CONTENT AREA(S):**   Cross-curricular

• To reinforce the concept of main idea or theme, have students design a book jacket or cover that depicts their understanding of the major idea of a book or story previously read.

**WHO:**               Elementary/Middle/High
**WHEN:**              During or after a lesson
**CONTENT AREA(S):**   Cross-curricular

• Have students design a poster that illustrates the major details of a specific concept or unit of study. For example, in science students could illustrate one of the eight planets along with written pertinent facts regarding the planet. In social studies, students could draw a picture depicting the climate, topography, and natural resources of a particular location being studied.

**WHO:**               Elementary/Middle/High
**WHEN:**              During a lesson
**CONTENT AREA(S):**   Social studies

• Have students select a particular culture or social group and make a collage, either by drawing or by collecting pictures, of the commonly held values, beliefs, traditions, and behaviors that are characteristic of the culture. As students display their collages, assist them in making comparisons between cultures and determining similarities and differences (Tate, 2012, p. 26).

**WHO:**               Elementary/Middle/High
**WHEN:**              During a lesson
**CONTENT AREA(S):**   Mathematics

• Give students a math word problem to read and then have them draw a series of pictures illustrating their understanding of what is actually happening in each step of the problem. Have them use the pictures to assist them in writing the numerical symbols for the word problem.

**WHO:**               Elementary/Middle/High
**WHEN:**              After a lesson
**CONTENT AREA(S):**   Science

- Have students draw and label the particular parts or processes of the human body, for example, the heart, lungs, digestive process, and so forth.

**WHO:**              Elementary/Middle/High
**WHEN:**             After a lesson
**CONTENT AREA(S):**  Social studies

- When students come in class, have a piece of butcher paper on one wall and markers available. Tell students that today they will design a class mural based on details that they remember from yesterday's class, such as, one thing they remember about the Harlem Renaissance. Have them draw on their spot on the mural and be prepared to explain to the class what they drew and why. Then allow students to view one another's pictures, which should help in their recall of information.

**WHO:**              Elementary/Middle/High
**WHEN:**             After a lesson
**CONTENT AREA(S):**  Science

- On a single sheet of paper, have students create a foldable booklet. An example of such a booklet can be seen at www.pocketmod.com. On the pages of the booklet, have students describe and draw (in rank order) the following: electron, proton, neutron, nucleus, atom, and molecule. This activity will rank orders by size and reinforce structure at the nanoscale (Tate & Phillips, 2011).

**WHO:**              Elementary/Middle/High
**WHEN:**             After a lesson
**CONTENT AREA(S):**  Mathematics

- Have students make drawings that will illustrate mathematical terms that have already been taught. These could include such terms as fraction, decimal, perpendicular lines, parallel lines, isosceles triangle, rhombus, radius, chord, and so forth.

**WHO:**              Elementary/Middle/High
**WHEN:**             During a lesson
**CONTENT AREA(S):**  Music

- Give students paper with the bass and treble clef lines and spaces already drawn in. Have them draw in the notes to represent a simple or complicated piece of music. Assist them in connecting the musical notation to the actual notes played on a keyboard or other musical instrument.

**WHO:**              Elementary/Middle/High
**WHEN:**             After a lesson
**CONTENT AREA(S):**  Social studies

• To assist students in recalling information regarding a person or group of people, have them draw a stick person symbol. Have them attach notes about the person or group in eight areas to the appropriate spot on the figure: ideas to the brain, hopes or vision to the eyes, words to the mouth, actions to the hands, feelings to the heart, movement to the feet, weaknesses to the Achilles tendon, and strengths to the arm muscle (Sousa, 2006).

**WHO:**                        Middle and High
**WHEN:**                       During a lesson
**CONTENT AREA(S):**            Mathematics

Have students create tessellations to apply their understandings of symmetry and transformations. A tessellation is a pattern of shapes that is repeated over and over and covers a specific area. The repeated shapes must fit together with no overlaps or gaps. Use students' tessellations to teach concepts of area, angles, length, congruency, and transformation.

## REFLECTION AND APPLICATION

How will I incorporate *drawing and artwork* into instruction to engage students' brains?

Which drawing and artwork activities am I already integrating as I teach the curriculum?

What additional activities will I integrate?

# Strategy 3

# Field Trips

## WHAT: DEFINING THE STRATEGY

Last April, I was invited to present for the Honolulu Association for Supervision and Curriculum Development. My husband and I went in one week earlier than the day on which I was to present so that we could enjoy the scenic beauty and historical significance of our 50th state. I will never forget spending one of those days at Pearl Harbor. We were there with several high school classes who experienced the same emotional impact on this field trip as did we. After a tour of the grounds and a video recalling the horrific attack on December 7, 1941, we were transported by boat to the *U.S.S. Arizona* Memorial. All of us tourists, including the students, disembarked the boat and realized that we were now standing over the remains of almost 1,000 service men whose bodies are still buried beneath the water since the ship was never raised after it was bombed. It was such a spiritual experience that no one said a word. Students did not even have to be told not to talk. They just didn't! As I read the names of each serviceman engraved on the wall, I shuddered with the thought that all of these brave men had given their lives in service to our country. We were later told that there was so much camaraderie on that ship, that many survivors of that day asked that their ashes be brought back to the water upon their deaths and deposited into the ocean with their fellow seamen.

The purpose of the brain is not to make good grades or to score high on standardized tests. The brain has but one purpose: survival in the real world. Students can read about Pearl Harbor, research it on the Internet, or view a video, but none of those things can serve as substitutes for the field trip the students and I took on that day. Is it any wonder that the places that you and your students travel to in the real world are long remembered? This would make the strategy of field trips one of the most unforgettable!

## WHY: THEORETICAL FRAMEWORK

Researchers at the University of Arkansas found that when students take field trips to cultural institutions, their critical-thinking skills, levels of tolerance, and historical empathy improve (Greene & Kisida, 2013).

"Much like babies who learn more by watching real people than by looking at two-dimensional screens, teenagers learn better from real humans, too" (Todd, 2014).

Field trips to live performances of plays enhance students' tolerance, literary knowledge, and empathy for what other people think and feel (University of Arkansas, 2014).

In a large-scale study of 11,000 students at more than 120 schools, research suggested that students retained a large amount of information from field trips taken and actually improved their critical-thinking skills. This was particularly the case with students from high-poverty schools (Greene & Kisida, 2013).

Since the field trip provides a real experience that makes content more relevant, it is a valuable and time-honored part of the social studies curriculum (Melber & Hunter, 2010).

Since electronic field trips expand the learning outside the walls of the classroom and enable students to experience an event more than once, they can be more beneficial than real-world field trips (Gregory & Herndon, 2010).

Because students need concrete, real-world examples and need to see, touch, and experience the world, a field trip can be a useful teaching tool prior to starting a teaching unit (Gregory & Parry, 2006).

Well-planned field trips are better than lab experiments in emulating good science because students formulate questions about nature, devise methods for answering the questions, implement the methods, evaluate the answers, and share the results with others (Davis, 2002).

Field trips, including those that are virtual, enable teachers to create as many authentic, experiential experiences as possible. These spatial memories are embedded in the brain and need no rehearsal (Fogarty, 2009).

Enhancing higher-order thinking skills, refining observation and questioning skills, and increasing the confidence and attitude of students are all benefits of field trips (Davis, 2002).

Aristotle and Socrates, two of the world's greatest teachers, used field trips thousands of years ago, as tools of instruction (Krepel & Duvall, 1981).

## HOW: INSTRUCTIONAL ACTIVITIES

**WHO:** Elementary/Middle/High
**WHEN:** Before a lesson
**CONTENT AREA(S):** Cross-curricular

• For a change of scenery, convene class outside of the classroom on the school grounds. Allowing students to absorb the vitamin D and other positive effects of sunlight and the beauty of nature calms students' brains and puts the mind in a good state for learning. Conducting a class discussion while sitting under a tree can add a whole new dimension to instruction.

**WHO:**                Elementary
**WHEN:**               During a lesson
**CONTENT AREA(S):**    Mathematics

• Field trips do not have to cost money. Use the school as well as the community for your field trip. Ask students to look for patterns in their environment such as in the stars and stripes on the American flag, clothing of classmates, the bricks in the school building, or the leaves on the trees. Point out the obvious way that objects, shapes, and colors are patterned in the real world.

**WHO:**                Elementary/Middle/High
**WHEN:**               After a lesson
**CONTENT AREA(S):**    Mathematics

• Following lessons on the concepts of angles, circles, rays, lines, line segments, and intersecting and parallel lines, take the class outside and have them identify these items on the sports fields or in the outside environment. Have students measure these fields. Following this field trip, lead students in a discussion of how geometry affects the design of sports fields (Tate, 2009).

**WHO:**                Elementary/Middle
**WHEN:**               Before a lesson
**CONTENT AREA(S):**    Science

• Prior to a unit of study on the solar system, have students visit a planetarium where they actually see replicas of what they will be studying, including the stars, planets, constellations, and so forth.

**WHO:**                Elementary/Middle/High
**WHEN:**               During a lesson
**CONTENT AREA(S):**    History

• Plan and take a field trip to a natural history or other type of museum to view exhibits and artifacts related to a unit of study. Visit the museum in advance and plan a scavenger hunt so that when students visit they can search for predetermined items and find the answers to prearranged questions.

**WHO:**                Elementary/Middle
**WHEN:**               During a lesson
**CONTENT AREA(S):**    Science

- To beautify the campus and learn about gardening, have students research, design, and plant a garden, butterfly garden, or water garden. Bulbs can be planted in the design of the school initials or logo. The more familiar names and more scientific names of the plants can be labeled. Have students plan and conduct tours for other classrooms that are visiting the garden (Tate & Phillips, 2011).

**WHO:**                Elementary/Middle/High
**WHEN:**               During a lesson
**CONTENT AREA(S):**    Cross-curricular

- Oftentimes, the classroom does not provide enough space for movement and games. Take the class outside and engage them in purposeful movement to reinforce a content objective or to play a game that requires more space than four walls will allow.

**WHO:**                Middle/High
**WHEN:**               During a lesson
**CONTENT AREA(S):**    Mathematics

- Have students walk around their community and create math problems from their environment based on what they are discovering as they walk around the neighborhood. Have them accompany their problems with the photographs, videos, or recordings essential for others to solve the problem.

**WHO:**                Elementary/Middle/High
**WHEN:**               During a lesson
**CONTENT AREA(S):**    Cross-curricular

- Thanks to virtual field trips, have students experience what it is like to visit locations of interest around the globe and never leave the classroom. Go online to websites and access virtual field trips that pertain to a concept being taught. For example, one such site for social studies is www.virtualfreesites.com/museums.html, a virtual library of museums from around the world.

**WHO:**                Elementary/Middle/High
**WHEN:**               After a lesson
**CONTENT AREA(S):**    Social studies

- Have students emulate the work of an ethnographer by observing and describing one area of the school, including the entrance to the building, the front office, the principal's office, the cafeteria, the halls when students are changing classes, and the media center. Have students, like the social scientist, gather data, select and interpret the relevant data, and reflect on the findings as well as the process of collection. Then have them write a description of what they have observed for a specific audience, such as students who will attend the school in 2020, a visitor from another country, or any other target audience they select (Melber & Hunter, 2010).

## REFLECTION AND APPLICATION

> ### How will I incorporate *field trips* into instruction to engage students' brains?

**Which field trip activities am I already integrating as I teach the curriculum?**

**What additional activities will I incorporate?**

# Strategy 4

# Games

## WHAT: DEFINING THE STRATEGY

As I travel around the United States presenting, I am realizing that the fun has gone out of teaching and learning in so many classrooms. With increased emphasis on standardized and criterion-referenced testing, benchmarks, and accountability, school is just not fun anymore! In the name of increased academic achievement, many school systems are even removing recess time from the students' school day. Fortunately, other school systems are doing just the opposite. They are recommending that students take their more difficult subjects immediately after they take physical education. As I taught in Singapore, whose students have some of the highest math scores in the world, I noticed that students were spending time learning math and then, just as importantly, stopping math instruction for recess.

While preschool children love to play games, it is also one of the 10 activities that keep people living beyond the age of 80 (Mahoney, 2005). There is even a pertinent saying: *You don't stop playing games because you grow old. You grow old because you stop playing games.* That would lead one to believe that games are beneficial throughout one's life and that elementary, middle, and high school students would benefit from spirited interaction in the pleasurable strategy of game playing. Not only is the strategy motivating, but it also can put students' brains in a positive state. When students hear their teacher say, *Let's play a game!*, the stress level is decreased and the retention rate for content increased. Boys, especially, are naturally motivated when a review is turned into a competition.

My family and I are constantly involved in game playing. My two daughters, son-in-law, and I are all evenly matched in our ability to play Scrabble. Many great evenings have been spent making words that are ripe for a challenge! My husband and I play Backgammon, and he enjoys a spirited game of chess. We have a whole game corner in our house and love to engage family members in Taboo, Pictionary, or Scattergories. Even though any of the following games can be computerized, when we play family games, all cell phones, iPads, and iPods disappear!

## WHY: THEORETICAL FRAMEWORK

Children pay more attention to academic tasks when brief, frequent opportunities for free play are provided (Dewar, 2008–2014).

Students today are used to playing personal computer and video games that give the student instant feedback and enable them to make adjustments that move them to the next level (Nash, 2012).

Having students develop a game to test one another on their knowledge of the content not only results in fun, but also forces students to rehearse and comprehend the concepts taught (Sousa, 2011).

Computer games allow students to receive the consequences of poor choices and enable them to try over and over again until they make the right one (Prensky, 2006).

Research suggests that the way in which children play contributes to their ability to creatively solve divergent problems, those to which there may be multiple solutions (Dewar, 2008–2014).

Using game formats encourages students to cooperate with one another, helps them focus and pay attention, and is motivating and loads of fun (Algozzine, Campbell, & Wang, 2009a).

When students develop a game's content as well as play the game, the amount of time they are exposed to and involved with the content is doubled (Allen, 2008).

Games are not only perfect for raising the level of feel-good amines in the brain but, in the correct amounts, games can also increase cognition and working memory (Jensen, 2007, p. 4).

Games such as *Wheel of Fortune* and *Jeopardy* provide students with great formats for remembering content (Caine, Caine, McClintic, & Klimek, 2005).

A ball-toss game not only encourages cooperation, problem solving, and physical movement, but it also enables students to think and act quickly while operating in a safe environment (Jensen, 2007).

Using an event in history, a model, or a game to explore the richness of math are some of the various ways teachers can teach specific math topics (Posamentier & Hauptman, 2006).

Students not only learn more when playing a game but their participation in class and their motivation for learning math increases (Posamentier & Jaye, 2006).

The need for survival, belonging and love, power, freedom, and fun are the five critical needs that must be satisfied if people are to be effectively motivated (Glasser, 1999).

# HOW: INSTRUCTIONAL ACTIVITIES

**WHO:**                          Elementary/Middle/High
**WHEN:**                         After a lesson
**CONTENT AREA(S):**              Cross-curricular

• Buy a generic game board, such as Candy Land, or have students work in cooperative groups to construct an original game board according to the following guidelines: The game must provide at least 30 spaces, including a *begin* and *end* space, two *move ahead* spaces, and two *go back* spaces. Have students make game question cards appropriate to whatever content needs to be reviewed with an accompanying answer key. Each group of students uses another group's game board and questions. Each group reviews content by rolling a number generator (die), moving the rolled number of spaces, selecting a card, and answering the designated question on the card. If the answer is correct, the student moves the rolled number of spaces. If the answer is incorrect, the student stays put. The first student in each group to get to the end of the game board wins.

**WHO:**                          Elementary/Middle
**WHEN:**                         After a lesson
**CONTENT AREA(S):**              Mathematics

• Following a lesson on factors, have students play the game SWITCH. Place a number on the document camera or SMART board, such as 36. Ask students to consider all of the factors of 36. Call out another number, such as 6. If the second number (6) is a factor of the pictured number (36), then students are given to the count of five to switch seats with another student in class. If by the count of five a student is not in another student's seat, that student is considered out of the game. If the second number is not a factor of the original number, then all students are to remain seated. If a student gets up when he or she shouldn't, that student is also out of the game. Give students several examples of numbers that are factors and not factors of the given number. Then change to another given number. I played this game with a group of fifth-graders recently, and we were laughing so hard we could hardly finish the game. Let me tell you one that always gets students out. The original number is 36. The second number is 13. Many students get up since they think 13 is a factor of 36. It is not!

**WHO:**                          Elementary/Middle
**WHEN:**                         After a lesson
**CONTENT AREA(S):**              Cross-curricular

• Have students make 15 matched pairs of content-area vocabulary words and their definitions. Have them write each word on one index card and the accompanying definition on another card. Have them spread the word and definition cards out face down in random order. Students work in pairs taking turns matching each word to its appropriate definition. One match entitles the student to another try. The student with the most matches at the end of the game wins.

| | |
|---|---|
| **WHO:** | Elementary/Middle |
| **WHEN:** | During or after a lesson |
| **CONTENT AREA(S):** | Mathematics |

• Have students work in pairs to become more automatic with addition facts. Give each pair a deck of cards. Have students deal the deck equally between the two of them. Have each student hold his or her half deck in his or her hand with the cards face down. Have them turn the top cards up simultaneously and add the value of the two cards together. For example, if one student turns over a 7 and another a 3, then the first student to say 10 gets both cards. Jacks are worth 11 points; queens are worth 12 points; and kings are worth 13 points. Aces can be worth either 1 point or 14 points. The first student to take all the cards or the one who has the most cards when the time is up is named the winner. You may want to pair students with like abilities together.

| | |
|---|---|
| **WHO:** | Elementary/Middle/High |
| **WHEN:** | After a lesson |
| **CONTENT AREA(S):** | Cross-curricular |

• Write each content-area vocabulary word on a different index card. Have students play Charades by taking turns coming to the front of the room, selecting a word card, and acting out the definition of the word. The student is not allowed to speak or write but must use gestures to act out the word. The first student in class to guess the word gets a point. The student with the most points at the end of the game is the winner.

| | |
|---|---|
| **WHO:** | Elementary/Middle/High |
| **WHEN:** | After a lesson |
| **CONTENT AREA(S):** | Cross-curricular |

• Play *Jeopardy* with the class by dividing them into three heterogeneous teams. Each team selects a team captain who gives the answers to the emcee and a scribe who keeps track of the points for the team and writes down the *Jeopardy* answer during the bonus round. Select key points from the chapter or unit of study and turn them into answers for the board. Five answers are placed into five columns of $100 increments, with the easiest answers worth $100 and the most difficult worth $500. Teams then compete against one another by taking turns selecting an answer and providing the appropriate question. If the answer is correct, the points are added to the score. If the answers are incorrect, the points are subtracted. Include two *daily doubles* to make the game more interesting. Play continues according to the rules of the television show until all of the answers have been selected. Any team with money can wager any or all of it during the *bonus round*. The bonus question should be one of the most difficult ones. The team with the most money at the end of the game wins. A computerized version of *Jeopardy* is available.

| | |
|---|---|
| **WHO:** | Elementary/Middle/High |
| **WHEN:** | After a lesson |
| **CONTENT AREA(S):** | Cross-curricular |

• Play *Wheel of Fortune* with the class by selecting a content-area vocabulary word previously taught. Place one line on the board for each letter in the chosen word. Have students take turns guessing letters of the alphabet that may be in the word. If the letter is in the word, write it on the correct line. If it is not, place the letter in a column off to the side. The first student to guess the word wins a point.

**Adaptation:** Have students work in pairs to select a word and have their partner guess the word. The student in each pair who guesses their word in the shortest amount of time is the winner.

| | |
|---|---|
| **WHO:** | Elementary/Middle/High |
| **WHEN:** | During a lesson |
| **CONTENT AREA(S):** | Cross-curricular |

• Have students participate in a People Search where they have to find answers to 12 short, unfinished statements in a 4 × 3 grid drawn on a piece of paper. The statements should reflect content that you would like for students to review. Students can supply only one answer for themselves. Then they must get the remaining 11 answers from 11 different classmates. Play some fast-paced music and have students walk around the classroom getting answers from their peers. As each peer provides an answer, they initial each student's paper indicating that they provided the answer. At the end of the song, students should have 12 different initials including their own and the answers to all 12 statements. Review the statements with the entire class to be sure that all students have the correct answers.

| | |
|---|---|
| **WHO:** | Middle/High |
| **WHEN:** | During a lesson |
| **CONTENT AREA(S):** | Cross-curricular |

• Have students play the Loop game by writing the statements and questions similar to the following on index cards and passing them out randomly to students in the class. Students then stand and read the answer if they have the card that answers another student's question.

- ○ **I have a right triangle.** Who has a triangle with all sides congruent?
- ○ **I have an equilateral triangle.** Who has the number of degrees in each of its angles?

- o **I have 60 degrees.** Who has the segment of a triangle from a vertex to the midpoint of the opposite side?
- o **I have median.** Who has a triangle with each angle less than 90 degrees?
- o **I have an acute triangle.** Who has a triangle with at least two congruent sides?
- o **I have an isosceles triangle.** Who has an equation whose graph is a line?
- o **I have a linear equation.** Who has the name of the side opposite the right angle in a right triangle?
- o **I have the hypotenuse.** Who has an equation for the area of a circle?
- o **I have a = πr².** Who has an equation that states that two ratios are equal?
- o **I have proportion.** Who has a quadrilateral with four congruent sides?

Students can write additional questions and answers that will form the basis of the remaining cards for playing this game. You should have as many cards as there are students in class (Bulla, 1996). This game can also be adapted to any content area by changing the answers and the questions.

**Adaptation:** This game can be made more fun by recording the time it takes to get through one cycle and then repeating the cycle two more times in an effort to beat the time. The repetition of hearing the answers more than once is good for students' brains.

| | |
|---|---|
| **WHO:** | Elementary/Middle/High |
| **WHEN:** | During a lesson |
| **CONTENT AREA(S):** | Cross-curricular |

• Provide students with a bingo sheet containing 25 blank spaces. Have students write previously taught, content-area vocabulary words randomly in any space on their cards. Then have students take turns randomly pulling from a bag and reading the definition of a designated word. Have students cover or mark out each word as the definition is read. The first student to cover five words in a row, horizontally, vertically, or diagonally, shouts out, "Bingo!" However, to win, the student must orally give the definition for the five words that comprise the *bingo*. If the student cannot supply the definitions, then play continues until a subsequent student wins.

**Adaptation:** Have students randomly write answers to math problems in the 25 blank spaces. Have students randomly pull and read math problems from the bag as students cover the correct answers.

| | |
|---|---|
| **WHO:** | Elementary/Middle/High |
| **WHEN:** | During a lesson |
| **CONTENT AREA(S):** | Language arts/History |

• Have students play the Who Am I? game by providing written clues regarding a famous literary or historical figure already studied. Have students take turns standing and reading their clues aloud as class members try to guess the identity of the figure. Any student who is the first to guess wins a point. If no one is able to identify the figure, then the student providing the clues gets the point.

**WHO:**                  Elementary/Middle/High
**WHEN:**             After a lesson
**CONTENT AREA(S):**   Cross-curricular

• Have students compete in pairs and take turns being the first to get their partners to guess a designated vocabulary word by providing them with a one-word synonym or clue for the word. No gestures are allowed. Bring two pairs of students to the front of the class and show one person in each pair the same word. One pair begins. If the word is missed, play reverts to the other pair. The point value begins at 10 and decreases by one each time the word is not guessed. If the word has not been guessed by the time the point value gets to five, then tell the word. Bring up two new pairs of students and a new word is given. This game is patterned after the television game show *Password*.

**WHO:**                  Elementary/Middle/High
**WHEN:**             During a lesson
**CONTENT AREA(S):**   Cross-curricular

• During a class discussion, when a question is asked, toss a Nerf or any other soft ball to the student who is to respond. The student gets one point for catching the ball and two points for answering the question correctly. If the student is correct, he or she can randomly pick the student who is to answer the next question and randomly toss the ball to that student. If the student answers incorrectly, he or she must toss the ball back to you so that you can select the next student. Be sure to ask the question of the entire class prior to selecting someone to catch the ball and answer the question.

**WHO:**                  Elementary/Middle/High
**WHEN:**             After a lesson
**CONTENT AREA(S):**   Cross-curricular

• Following a unit of study and prior to a test, have students work in heterogeneous groups to write 10 questions regarding the content at varying levels of difficulty with four possible answer choices. Each question is assigned a monetary level of difficulty in $100 increments, ranging from $100 to $1,000. Have them also write three additional difficult questions worth $5,000, $25,000, and $100,000, respectively. Have student groups compete to earn money for their team by answering another team's questions. This game is adapted from the television game show, *Who Wants to Be a Millionaire?*

**WHO:**                     Elementary/Middle/High
**WHEN:**                    During a lesson
**CONTENT AREA(S):**         Cross-curricular

• Encourage students to review appropriate content-area vocabulary by playing Pictionary. Divide the class into two heterogeneous teams. Students from each team take turns coming to the front of the room, pulling a vocabulary word from a box, and drawing a picture on the board that will get their team members to say the word before time is called. No words may be spoken. If the team succeeds in guessing the word within a specific time limit (such as 15 seconds), the team gets one point. The team with the most points when all words have been used is the winner.

**WHO:**                     Elementary/Middle/High
**WHEN:**                    During a lesson
**CONTENT AREA(S):**         Cross-curricular

• Purchase the CD, *Classic TV Game Show Themes*, so that you have the music that accompanies many of the games that you will play with your class. The CD has the themes from the following game shows: *Wheel of Fortune, Jeopardy, Password, Family Feud, The Price Is Right,* and many more.

**WHO:**                     Elementary/Middle
**WHEN:**                    During a lesson
**CONTENT AREA(S):**         Cross-curricular

• Consult the series *Engage the Brain Games* for a plethora of additional game ideas across the curriculum. Books for kindergarten through Grade 5 are cross-curricula, including games in the content areas of language arts, math, science, social studies, music, and physical education. There is a separate book in language arts, mathematics, science, and social studies for Grades 6 through 8. Consult the Corwin website at www.corwinpress .com for information.

REFLECTION AND APPLICATION

> ## How will I incorporate *games* into
> ## instruction to engage students' brains?

**Which games am I already integrating as I teach the curriculum?**

**What additional activities will I integrate?**

# Strategy 5

# Graphic Organizers, Semantic Maps, and Word Webs

## WHAT: DEFINING THE STRATEGY

I was teaching a fourth-grade language arts class where the objective was to have students make inferences regarding the elements of fiction and identify the traits of fictional characters. The story was *The Hundred Dresses* by Eleanor Estes. The three major characters are Peggy, Maddie, and Wanda, whose character traits are quite different. Peggy can be considered a bully who, along with Maddie, finds ways to embarrass shy, timid Wanda and her claim that, even though she is of low socioeconomic status, she has 100 dresses at home. After reading the story in a variety of ways, including oral, partner, choral, and cloze reading, I had students work with a partner to complete the Character Traits graphic organizer below. Students then had to go back to the text and find evidence to support each identified trait.

Whether referred to as concept, mind, or semantic maps or as word webs, graphic organizers are one of the best friends of a teacher who desires to facilitate the comprehension of students. Graphic organizers address both the left and the right hemispheres of students' brains, so they are beneficial to all. The students strong in left hemisphere can supply the verbiage, and the right-hemisphere students have the option of showing what they know pictorially. Having students draw the organizer along with you as you explain the major concepts and details facilitates memory.

# WHY: THEORETICAL FRAMEWORK

Graphic organizers can help students organize and use information by processing random thoughts and pulling them together (Gregory & Chapman, 2013).

When visual patterns are shown through graphic representations, a 49-percentile point gain can be achieved (Tileston & Darling, 2009).

Graphic organizers are visual, spatial, mathematical, and logical tools that enable students to organize information so that they can see their thinking (Gregory & Chapman, 2013).

When students write study notes, if they include graphics that correspond to the symbols on a class mind map, their memory of the notes will be facilitated (Allen & Scozzi, 2012).

Concept maps help students synthesize and recognize major themes, ideas, and interrelationships, especially for those students who do not possess organizing and synthesizing skills (Hattie, 2009).

Graphic organizers make abstract ideas more visible and concrete and can make connections between a student's prior knowledge, what they are learning today, and what they can apply to future learning (Burke, 2009).

"Graphic organizers make thinking and learning visible" (Fogarty, 2009, p. 112).

Graphic organizers enable English language learners to organize words and ideas in a way which helps them see patterns and relationships in mathematics (Coggins et al., 2007).

Graphic organizers represent a form of *nonlinguistic representation* and are one of the most popular ways teachers can have students represent the knowledge that they have experienced (Marzano, 2007, p. 52).

Graphic organizers provide a creative alternative to rote memorization since they enable students to make connections, access previously stored memories, and see patterns, which all nurture brain growth (Willis, 2006).

Flow charts, continuums, matrices, Venn diagrams, concept maps, and problem-solution charts are all types of graphic representations that can be used by mathematics teachers because they can be quickly understood and can provide structure for synthesizing new information (Posamentier & Jaye, 2006).

The visual displays that concept maps provide facilitate the reading comprehension and recall of students who have difficulty learning since it helps them organize verbal information (Kim, Vaugh, Wanzek, & Wei, 2004).

According to the Institute for the Advancement of Research in Education (IARE), 29 scientifically based research studies support the use of graphic organizers for improving student achievement across all grade levels, content areas, and with diverse student populations (IARE, 2003).

# Character Traits

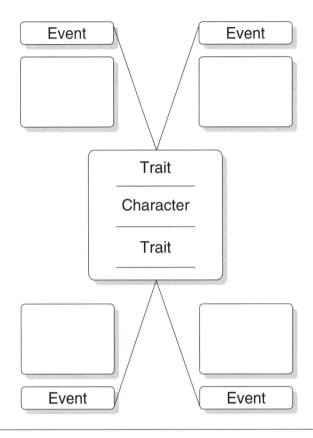

Figure 5.1

## HOW: INSTRUCTIONAL ACTIVITIES

**WHO:** Elementary/Middle/High
**WHEN:** Before and after a lesson
**CONTENT AREA(S):** All

• To access students' prior knowledge and summarize content after a lesson is taught, have students complete a K-N-L graphic organizer. Have students discuss or brainstorm (1) what they already *know* about a concept or unit of study; (2) what they will *need* to know to comprehend the concept, and (3) following instruction, what they have *learned*.

# The K-N-L Strategy

| Topic: | | |
|---|---|---|
| *What I Know* | *What I Need to Know* | *What I Learned* |
| | | |
| | | |
| | | |
| | | |
| | | |
| | | |

Figure 5.2

**WHO:**                Elementary/Middle/High
**WHEN:**               During a lesson
**CONTENT AREA(S):**    Cross-curricular

• Because the brain thinks in chunks or connections, have students increase their knowledge of vocabulary by using a word web. As new vocabulary is introduced, have students complete the word web below by brainstorming additional synonyms for the new word. Students can keep their word webs in a notebook for review and add synonyms throughout the year. Encourage them to add these words to their speaking and writing vocabularies as well.

# Vocabulary Word Web

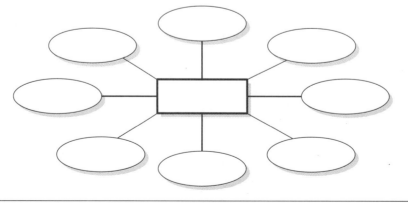

Figure 5.3

**WHO:**                          Elementary/Middle/High
**WHEN:**                         After a lesson
**CONTENT AREA(S):**              Cross-curricular

• After the reading of a story or novel where problems exist that must be resolved, have students complete the following story frame to demonstrate their understanding of the story's plot.

# Story Map

Title _____

Setting

Characters _____  _____

_____  _____

_____  _____

Problem:

Event 1 _____

Event 2 _____

Event 3 _____

Event 4 _____

Solution

**Figure 5.4**

**WHO:**              Elementary/Middle/High
**WHEN:**             During a lesson
**CONTENT AREA(S):**  Cross-curricular

• To help students identify the main idea and details in narrative or content-area texts, use the simile that a main idea and details are like a table top and legs. Draw a table with legs like the one below and have students write the main idea on the top of the table and one supporting detail on each leg.

# Main Idea Organizer

**Main Idea**

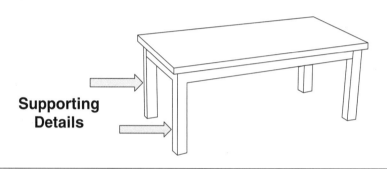

**Supporting
Details**

Figure 5.5

**WHO:**              Elementary/Middle/High
**WHEN:**             During or after a lesson
**CONTENT AREA(S):**  Cross-curricular

• Using the following graphic organizer, have students complete a **5Ws *and an H*** chart to ask and answer *who, what, when, where, why,* and *how* questions regarding either narrative or informational texts. Students should go into the text and look for specific text-dependent answers (Tate, 2014a, p. 51).

# "5Ws and an H"

Use the organizer below to create a "5Ws and an H" summary.

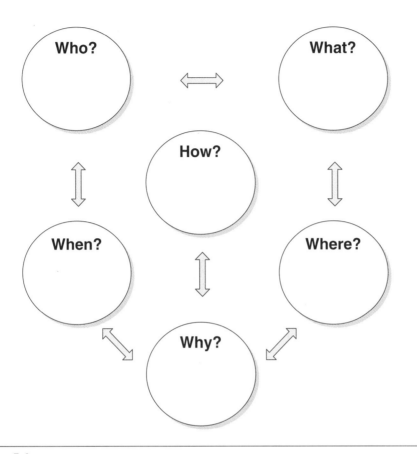

**Figure 5.6**

| | |
|---|---|
| **WHO:** | Elementary/Middle/High |
| **WHEN:** | During a lesson |
| **CONTENT AREA(S):** | Cross-curricular |

• Have students use one or more of the following visual organizers to assist them in understanding the basic formats of text structure (Strong, Silver, Perini, & Tuculescu, 2002).

# Cause/Effect Organizer

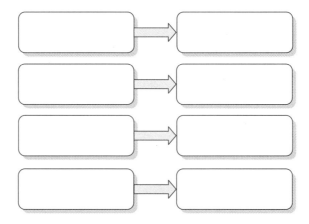

Figure 5.7

# Comparison Organizer

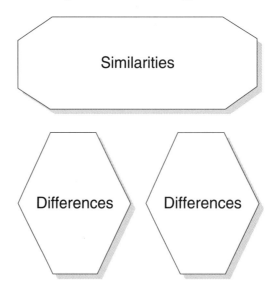

Figure 5.8

# Cycle Organizer

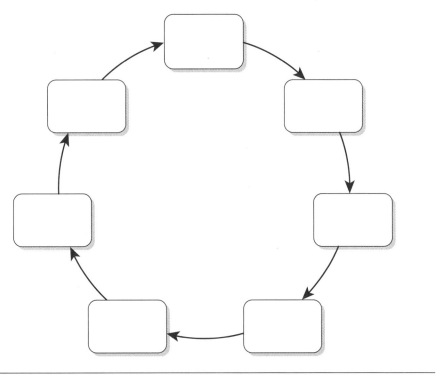

Figure 5.9

# Sequence Organizer

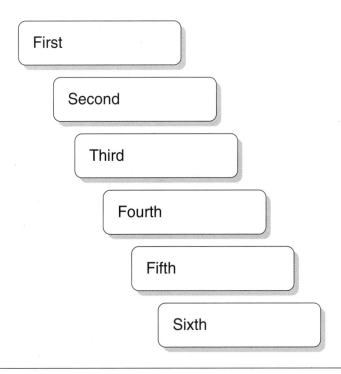

Figure 5.10

# Topic Description Organizer

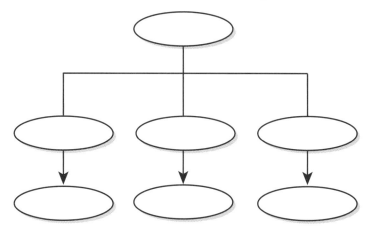

Figure 5.11

# Problem/Solution Organizer

| Problem | Solution | Effect |
|---------|----------|--------|
|  |  |  |
|  |  |  |
|  |  |  |
|  |  |  |

Figure 5.12

# Compare/Contrast Organizer

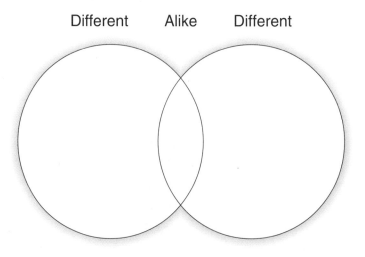

Figure 5.13

**WHO:**               Elementary/Middle/High
**WHEN:**              Before, during, or after a lesson
**CONTENT AREA(S):**   Cross-curricular

• While lecturing or discussing informational text with students, complete a semantic, concept, or mind map on the board as a visual of how the major concepts are related to one another. Have students copy the map in their notes as you explain each part. See the sample format in Figure 5.14.

# Mind Map

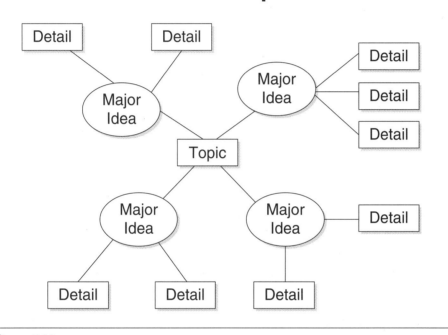

**Figure 5.14**

**WHO:**               Elementary/Middle/High
**WHEN:**              During a lesson
**CONTENT AREA(S):**   Cross-curricular

• While lecturing or discussing ideas with students, complete a semantic, concept, or mind map on the board to show how the major concepts are related to one another. Have students copy the map in their notes as you explain each part. The mind map below is completed by participants in my workshops as I teach them five ways to grow dendrites, or brain cells, in their students' brains.

# The Neuron

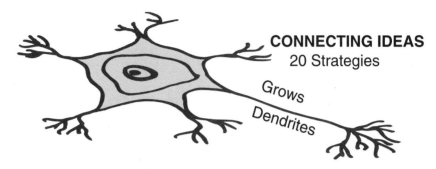

**TALKING**

- Sends oxygen
- Helps memory

**MOVING**

Procedural memory → strongest

**CONNECTING IDEAS**

20 Strategies

*Grows Dendrites*

**HAVING A PURPOSE**

- Make content relevant
- Stay active

**THINKING POSITIVELY**

Confidence

Threat

Anger    Fear

Stress

**Figure 5.15**

| | |
|---|---|
| **WHO:** | Elementary/Middle/High |
| **WHEN:** | After a lesson |
| **CONCEPT AREA(S):** | Cross-curricular |

- Once you have demonstrated how to do so, encourage students to create their own semantic, concept, or mind maps regarding a unit of study. This technique alone will enhance comprehension because these mind maps can be reviewed prior to testing to facilitate long-term retention.

| | |
|---|---|
| **WHO:** | Elementary/Middle |
| **WHEN:** | Before, during, and after a lesson |
| **CONCEPT AREA(S):** | Cross-curricular |

- Refer to the series Engage the Brain: Graphic Organizers and Other Visual Strategies to find additional graphic organizers in the content areas of language arts, math, science, and social studies. Grades K–5 have all content areas contained in the same book. Grades 6–8 have separate books for each of the four content areas. Consult the Corwin website at www .corwinpress.com for information.

## REFLECTION AND APPLICATION

> How will I incorporate *graphic organizers, semantic maps, and word webs* into instruction to engage students' brains?

Which graphic organizers, semantic maps, and word webs am I already integrating as I teach the curriculum?

What additional activities will I integrate?

# Strategy 6

# Humor

## WHAT: DEFINING THE STRATEGY

Four women were riding down the highway. The car was moving extremely slowly. A police officer saw them and decided to pull them over. He noticed that the driver was very calm but the three passengers were in a high state of stress. Their hair was sticking up on top of their heads and their clothes were disheveled. The police officer emphatically informed the driver that she was going too slowly. "No I wasn't," she replied. "I was doing exactly what the sign says. The sign says 28. I was driving 28 miles per hour." The police officer replied, "That is not the speed limit sign. That is the highway sign. You are on Highway 28." "I am so sorry! I got confused!" the woman replied apologetically. The police officer noticed that the three women were still shaking so he told them not to worry. He was not going to take the driver to jail or give her a ticket. "I will just give her a warning and let you all go on your way," the officer said. The driver commented to the police officer, "These ladies will be alright after a while. You see, we just got off of Highway 131!"

This is one joke I tell in my workshops. If it made you laugh or even smile, it put your brain in a more positive state. Research (Allen, 2008; Jensen, 2007) tells us that jokes, riddles, celebrations, and other forms of positive interaction not only create a positive learning environment but may also facilitate the learning itself.

Did you know that the brain does not know the difference between real laughter and fake laughter? You can fake laughter and it will have the same positive effect on the brain. That is why there are more than 1,800 laughing clubs in India alone.

Please do not confuse the use of humor in the classroom with sarcasm, which has the exact opposite effect on the brains of students. The literal definition of sarcasm is "a tearing of the flesh," aptly named because remarks directed to students that demean, tease, or deride can, at minimum, hinder or incapacitate higher-level thinking (Jensen, 1995).

## WHY: THEORETICAL FRAMEWORK

When students are laughing, they are releasing transmitters called endorphins, and laughter has been described as *the shortest distance between two people* (Gregory & Chapman, 2013, p. 24).

It is possible for learning to be both rigorous and enjoyable (Cooper & Garner, 2012).

Laughter produces endorphins, which stimulate the frontal lobes of students' brains and increase their levels of attention and degree of focus (Sousa, 2011).

Kinesthetic actions in the form of cheers can send more oxygen and glucose to the brain, resulting in the laughter that can raise endorphin levels (Gregory & Chapman, 2013).

When students laugh together, a diverse population bonds, community spirit forms, and a classroom climate becomes more conducive to learning (Sousa, 2011).

"What we learn with pleasure, we never forget" (Allen, 2008, p. 99).

Improvisational comedy enables students to think on their feet, puts a bit of fun and laughter into a lesson, and encourages students to take risks in front of their peers (Udvari-Solner & Kluth, 2008).

When students are stressed and perceive their learning environment as negative, cortisol is produced, which interferes with the recall of emotional memories (Kuhlmann, Kirschbaum, & Wolf, 2005).

Having laughter breaks in class increases the flow of positive neurotransmitters, which are necessary for alertness and memory (Jensen, 2007).

Humor has been found to free a person's creativity and to foster higher-level thinking skills, such as perceiving and anticipating novel situations, creating visual images, and forming analogies (Costa, 2008).

When students are experiencing minimal stress, levels of cognition are increased and information is allowed to flow more freely through the amygdala, the seat of emotion (Willis, 2007b).

Older adolescents are more apt to understand the subtleties of humor, satire, or irony since their language skills are more highly developed than those of younger students (Feinstein, 2004).

The use of humor is 1 of 12 intelligent behaviors, labeled as *habits of mind*. These *habits* are based on the premise that all students can be taught a set of skills that enable them to behave in intelligent ways (Costa, 1991).

# HOW: INSTRUCTIONAL ACTIVITIES

**WHO:**                    Elementary/Middle/High
**WHEN:**                   Before a lesson
**CONTENT AREA(S):**        Cross-curricular

• Have teachers in a grade level or a department form a laughing club. Since the brain does not know the difference between real laughter and fake laughter, these clubs appear to work. The laughing club can meet before school long enough for a teacher to share a joke or riddle with the members. Teachers can take turns bringing the jokes for the week. Everyone gets his or her day off to a positive start that can carry over into instruction.

**WHO:**                          Elementary/Middle/High
**WHEN:**                        Before a lesson
**CONTENT AREA(S):**    Cross-curricular

• To create an environment conducive to optimal learning, place humorous signs around the room. For example, one sign could say, *Knowledge given away here, free. Bring your own container* (Burgess, 2000, p. 20). Another sign could be *The longer you sit, the dumber you get!* (Tate, 2014b) or *Success comes in cans, not in can'ts!* (Tate, 2014b).

**WHO:**                          Elementary/Middle/High
**WHEN:**                        Before a lesson
**CONTENT AREA(S):**    Cross-curricular

• As you stand at the door to greet your class daily, *SMILE! SMILE* is a mnemonic device that stands for <u>S</u>how <u>M</u>e <u>I</u>'m <u>L</u>oved <u>E</u>veryday! Many students come in under threat, or high stress, and just a smiling teacher can help to change the state of their brains from negative to positive. After all, the brain learns best when it is not in high stress! On those days that you don't feel like smiling, get a *Smile on a Stick!* Go to www.humorproject .com and purchase a smile connected to a stick. Put the smile up to your mouth as you greet students. The smiles come in several varieties and are good for a hearty laugh from your students!

**WHO:**                          Elementary/Middle/High
**WHEN:**                        Before a lesson
**CONTENT AREA(S):**    Cross-curricular

• Don't take yourself or your students too seriously. Most students love a teacher who is able to make fun of herself. One high school teacher related to me how much his students love him, mostly due to his sense of humor. For example, when he teaches about plate tectonics, a shifting of the earth's plates, he tells students that there is a place in Africa where the plates collide. It is called Djibouti (jih-BOOT-ee). He told me that by the time they get through discussing the cracks in Djibouti, everybody remembers. If you don't get that joke, think about it a little longer! Remember to laugh with your students, but not at them!

**WHO:**                          Elementary (Primary Grades)
**WHEN:**                        Before, during, or after a lesson
**CONTENT AREA(S):**    Cross-curricular

- The brains of primary students are not developed enough to understand the subtleties of a joke. However, they enjoy riddles. I actually like riddles better than jokes for the brain. Students have to think at high cognitive levels to solve a riddle. Find some riddles that would be appropriate for this age level. Here are a few to get you started:

*Why did the turtle cross the road? Answer: To get to the Shell Station*

*Why don't the circus lions eat the circus clowns? Answer: Because they taste funny*

*What did one strawberry say to the other strawberry? Answer: If you weren't so fresh we wouldn't be in this jam (Tate, 2014b).*

| | |
|---|---|
| **WHO:** | Middle/High |
| **WHEN:** | Before, during, or after a lesson |
| **CONTENT AREA(S):** | Cross-curricular |

- Almost every middle and high school classroom has a class clown. Use that student to your advantage. Have them bring in jokes and/or riddles to tell to the class. Make sure you approve of each joke before it is shared. Either before class, during the last few minutes, or at appropriate times during the period, have the class clown tell a joke. The entire class will laugh, putting each brain in a positive state for learning. The job of the class clown can rotate to other volunteers in the class each week until every student who wants a turn has had one. The comedian Jim Carrey told the true story of one of his high school teachers who told Jim that if he participated in class and completed all of his homework, the last two minutes of class daily belonged to him. Needless to say, that deal ended up being a win-win for both parties!

| | |
|---|---|
| **WHO:** | Elementary/Middle/High |
| **WHEN:** | During a lesson |
| **CONTENT AREA(S):** | Cross-curricular |

- As you teach, locate or create and incorporate cartoons, riddles, and jokes that reinforce concepts you are teaching into the delivery of instruction.

| | |
|---|---|
| **WHO:** | Middle/High |
| **WHEN:** | After a lesson |
| **CONTENT AREA(S):** | Cross-curricular |

- Have students create jokes or riddles regarding a concept previously taught. The creation of jokes not only reinforces students' conceptual understanding but also encourages students to use their higher-level thinking skills. One math student created this original riddle. *Why did the fraction 1/5 go to the psychiatrist? Answer: He was just too tense (2/10).* Another original student thought up this riddle: *Why do you never want to say 288 in front of anyone? Answer: It is just too (two) gross!*

| **WHO:** | Middle/High |
|---|---|
| **WHEN:** | Before or during a lesson |
| **CONTENT AREA(S):** | Cross-curricular |

• Have students bring in riddles to share with the class. Read over each riddle and place the ones you approve in a *riddle box*. At the beginning of class or periodically throughout the period, stop and read a riddle from the box. Give points to the first student who can come up with the answer. The student who brought in the riddle is not allowed to guess but gets points for bringing in the riddle and extra points if no student can come up with the answer in an allotted time.

| **WHO:** | Elementary/Middle/High |
|---|---|
| **WHEN:** | After a lesson |
| **CONTENT AREA(S):** | Cross-curricular |

• Use humorous ways to randomly involve students in lessons. When students are working in cooperative groups and it is time to select a spokesperson for the group, have students point into the air. Then, on the count of three, have them point to the person in their group they want to be the spokesperson. The student with the most fingers pointing at him or her becomes the spokesperson. This activity always gets a hearty laugh!

| **WHO:** | Elementary/Middle/High |
|---|---|
| **WHEN:** | Before a lesson |
| **CONTENT AREA(S):** | Cross-curricular |

• Select students to fulfill a variety of roles in cooperative groups according to humorous categories such as the following:

  o Students wearing red (or any other color)
  o Students wearing contacts or glasses
  o Students with the longest/shortest hair (The hair does not have to be theirs.)
  o Students wearing the most jewelry, such as rings or earrings
  o Students who have the most brothers, sisters, or pets
  o Students who live closest to or farthest from school

| **WHO:** | Middle/High |
|---|---|
| **WHEN:** | After a lesson |
| **CONTENT AREA(S):** | Mathematics |

• The National Council of Teachers of Math (NCTM) knew the power of humor almost 50 years ago. They published a book in 1970 called *Mathematics and Humor*, where every joke, riddle, or pun taught a math concept. If you can retrieve a copy of this book, you will have a rich resource for incorporating humor into your math instruction. The cartoon below depicts an example.

**Figure 6.1**

| | |
|---|---|
| **WHO:** | Middle/High |
| **WHEN:** | During a lesson |
| **CONTENT AREA(S):** | Cross-curricular |

• Locate editorial or other cartoons that emphasize cross-curricular concepts already taught. Display them in class and have students use their higher-level thinking skills to explain the concept displayed in the cartoon. For older students, you may want to display the cartoon omitting the caption and have students work individually or in groups to create their own captions. You would be surprised how your students' original captions may be superior to the ones provided in the cartoons.

| | |
|---|---|
| **WHO:** | Elementary/Middle/High |
| **WHEN:** | During a lesson |
| **CONTENT AREAS:** | Cross-curricular |

• Provide positive feedback for appropriate student responses in humorous ways, such as providing applause with a plastic hand clapper, sending positive energy with a *positive energy stick* (magic wand), or blowing a paper horn.

| | |
|---|---|
| **WHO:** | Elementary/Middle/High |
| **WHEN:** | During a lesson |
| **CONTENT AREA(S):** | Cross-curricular |

• Have students support and celebrate appropriate answers given by peers. These might include, but are not limited to, clapping, high-fives, thumbs-up, or any of the following affirmations:

  ○ *Fantastic! Fantastic!* Student place their hands on either side of their faces and fan their faces as they say, *Fantastic! Fantastic!*
  ○ *Seal of Approval!* Students extend their arms, turn their palms outward, clapping and make a noise like a seal.
  ○ *WOW!* Students make a *W* by sticking up the three middle fingers of the right hand and the three middle fingers of the left hand and placing them on either side of the mouth which is formed in an *O*.

Consult Strategy 16, "Celebrate Good Times, Come On!," of the book *Shouting Won't Grow Dendrites: 20 Techniques to Detour Around the Danger Zones* (2nd ed.) for more than 30 additional ways to celebrate student success in the classroom (Tate, 2014b).

**WHO:**                            Elementary/Middle/High
**WHEN:**                        After a lesson
**CONTENT AREA(S):**      Cross-curricular

• Play games with students to review content prior to a test. Consult Strategy 4 ("Games") for numerous examples for involving students in a fun class with lots of laughter.

## REFLECTION AND APPLICATION

> How will I incorporate *humor* into
> instruction to engage students' brains?

**Which humorous activities am I already integrating as I teach the curriculum?**

**What additional activities will I integrate?**

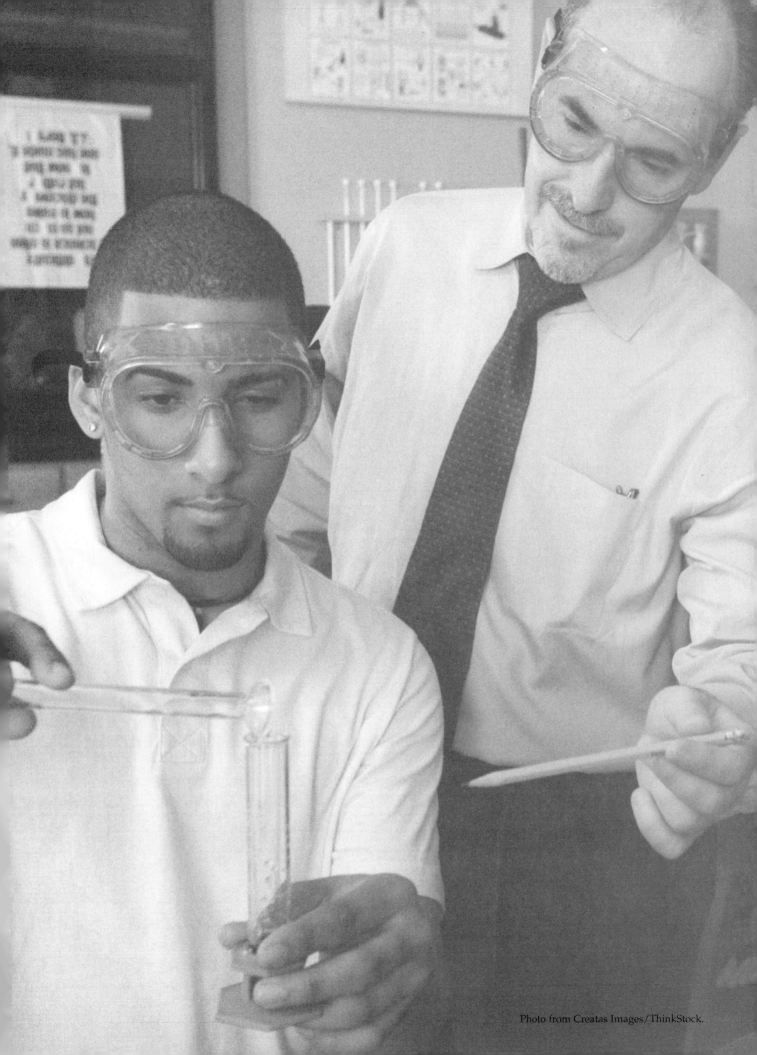

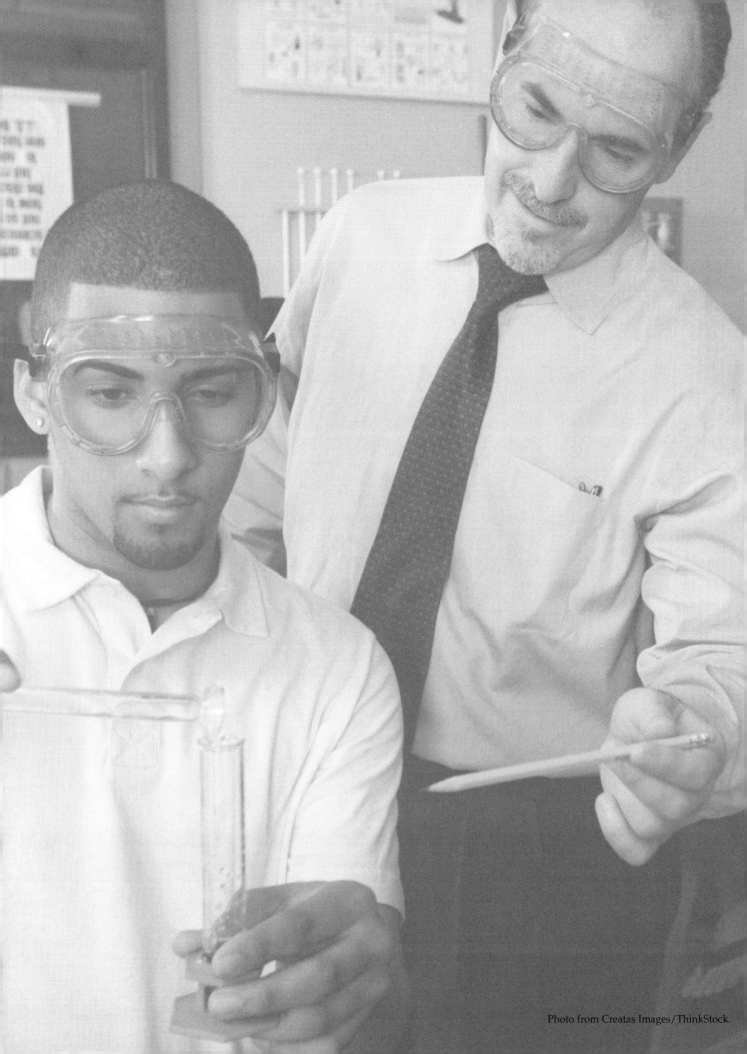

# Strategy 7

# Manipulatives, Experiments, Labs, and Models

## WHAT: DEFINING THE STRATEGY

I show the most adorable picture in my workshops of a first-grade classroom where students are busy working in cooperative groups to paste macaroni on strips of cardboard. The macaroni is to be pasted in a sequence of designated patterns, which is a predecessor to algebra. Every student in the class is hard at work using his or her hands to demonstrate their knowledge of patterning in math. By the way, the teacher has her iPod in the forefront of the picture to show me that while her students are working, they are listening to calming music. She related to me that her discipline problems have decreased by at least 50% since she started using music while students are working quietly. See Strategy 11 for research on music and the brain.

The use of the hands and brain activity are so complicated and interconnected that no one theory explains it (Jensen, 2001). I cannot explain it either! I just know that some students need to have their hands involved before their brains can understand. My son, Christopher, was one of those students. He had difficulty paying attention in class when his teachers lectured for the majority of the period. However, this was the same person who, as a teenager, could spend hours in his room constructing a moving Ferris wheel out of K'nex blocks or who excelled in a summer hands-on science camp sponsored by Georgia Institute of Technology. In fact, two of my three children, and many others like them, probably possess what Howard Gardner (1983) called visual-spatial intelligence. These students usually excel with hands-on strategies, such as using manipulatives or graphing calculators, conducting experiments, or constructing models, and teachers would do well to incorporate this strategy into their repertoire.

## WHY: THEORETICAL FRAMEWORK

Multiple props can be used at the beginning or throughout a lesson to create a memory hook to the content (Allen & Scozzi, 2012).

A mathematics meta-analysis shows that the greatest effects of aids such as calculators, manipulatives, and graphing aids happen when the aids reduce cognitive load and provide feedback between student and teacher (Hattie, 2009).

Teachers should provide students with manipulatives and have students engaged in holding and molding clay or other objects (Jensen, 2008).

When students are working with concrete shapes, they are developing the foundation for spatial sense (Wall & Posamentier, 2006).

Students' understanding of mathematical ideas is broadened when concrete representations are used (Coggins et al., 2007).

Manipulatives are valuable resources for assisting even high school students in accelerating their mathematical ability (Curtain-Phillips, 2008).

When learning is active and hands-on, the formation of neural connections is facilitated and information is much more readily remembered than information learned from an abstract viewpoint, where the teacher is doing the work while the students watch (Gregory & Parry, 2006).

Because concrete materials assist English language learners in focusing on new concepts and vocabulary at the same time, they are a crucial part of the instruction in fluency with mathematics (Coggins et al., 2007).

When students use manipulatives over a long period, they make gains in verbalizing their thinking, discussing ideas, taking ownership, and gaining confidence in independently finding answers to problems (Sebesta & Martin, 2004).

Manipulatives provide a strong foundation for students mastering concepts in measurement, decimals, percentages, probability, statistics, and number relations (Access Center, 2004).

Students in the early grades should be allowed to use manipulatives for as long as the students feel they are needed (Checkley, 1999).

## HOW: INSTRUCTIONAL ACTIVITIES

**WHO:**                          Elementary
**WHEN:**                         During a lesson
**CONTENT AREA(S):**              Cross-curricular

• Have students practice spelling or content-area vocabulary words in a number of tactile ways, including the following: writing the words in the air, writing them in shaving cream spread on the desk (a side benefit of this activity is that you end up with a clean desk when the activity ends), forming the words with clay or other pliable materials, or using magnetic alphabet letters to build the words.

| | |
|---|---|
| **WHO:** | Elementary |
| **WHEN:** | During a lesson |
| **CONTENT AREA(S):** | Mathematics |

• Give students pieces of construction paper and ask them to place the pieces in the shape of a pizza. Some students have two pieces, some four pieces, and some have eight pieces, all which form a whole pizza. Have students assemble the pieces of their pizza and then compare the sizes of their pieces with other classmates. Ask them to make assumptions regarding the sizes of the pieces, becoming familiar with terms such as halves, thirds, fourths, and eighths.

**Adaptation:** Instead of a pizza, give students a hamburger with all of the condiments cut out of round circles. The burger is on brown construction paper and is divided into halves, the cheese on top is on yellow paper and is in thirds, the red tomato is in fourths, the green pickle is in fifths, and the white onion is in sixths. The hamburger is set between two buns and enables students to see that although each part of the hamburger is in different fractional pieces, each piece adds up to the whole circle.

| | |
|---|---|
| **WHO:** | Elementary/Middle/High |
| **WHEN:** | During a lesson |
| **CONTENT AREA(S):** | Cross-curricular |

• Have students respond with manipulatives when answering questions in class. These response items can be in the form of cards, a dry-erase board that can be erased with a sock that students bring from home, or discarded copy paper. Have students write down short answers to selected questions asked in class. The objective of this activity is to have all students respond simultaneously and immediately assess students' understanding and retention (Tate, 2012).

| | |
|---|---|
| **WHO:** | Elementary/Middle/High |
| **WHEN:** | During a lesson |
| **CONTENT AREA(S):** | Mathematics |

• Place manipulatives, such as tiles, blocks, or Cuisenaire rods, on the document camera as you teach so students have a visual example of how they can use manipulatives to demonstrate a concept being taught.

| | |
|---|---|
| **WHO:** | Elementary/Middle/High |
| **WHEN:** | During a lesson |
| **CONTENT AREA(S):** | Mathematics |

• Have students use manipulatives, such as Unifix cubes, tiles, blocks, Cuisenaire rods, miniature clocks, or geoboards during mathematics instruction to display their understanding of a particular concept taught.

**WHO:**                Elementary/Middle/High
**WHEN:**               During a lesson
**CONTENT AREA(S):**    Science

• Design a laboratory experiment for students and allow them to follow specific directions to complete the experiment, demonstrating their understanding of a science concept being taught. For example, Warren Phillips conducts this experiment when he teaches his science workshop. Get an entire roll of Mentos and a two-liter bottle of diet cola. Unwrap the entire roll of Mentos and position them directly over the mouth of the bottle of diet cola so that all of the candies can drop into the bottle simultaneously. $CO_2$ will be released, sending the soda about 10 feet in the air. Have students come up and try varying numbers of Mentos, measuring eruption heights and times. This experiment is best done outdoors. Be sure that students have goggles and a lab apron (Tate & Phillips, 2011).

**WHO:**                Elementary/Middle/High
**WHEN:**               During a lesson
**CONTENT AREA(S):**    Language arts

• Give students small sticky notes. As they locate text evidence to support an author's point of view or make inferences, have students put the sticky notes on specific references in the book so that they can be easily located during small-group or whole-class discussion.

**WHO:**                Elementary/Middle/High
**WHEN:**               After a lesson
**CONTENT AREA(S):**    Cross-curricular

• Have students construct models that show their understanding of a concept previously taught. For example, have students construct a model of the solar system that shows the planets in order from the sun—from Mercury to Neptune, or have students construct a model of a home to scale with all of the necessary rooms and fixtures.

**WHO:**                Elementary/Middle/High
**WHEN:**               During a lesson
**CONTENT AREA(S):**    Cross-curricular

• Have students use their hands to show agreement or disagreement with an answer or level of understanding for an answer by doing one of the following:

   o Thumbs-up if you agree
   o Thumbs-down if you disagree

- o Five fingers if you completely understand
- o One finger if you don't understand
- o Pat head if you understand
- o Scratch head if you don't understand

**WHO:**                      Elementary/Middle/High
**WHEN:**                     Before and after a lesson
**CONTENT AREA(S):**          Cross-curricular

- Engage students in the Sort and Report activity according to the following guidelines: (1) Pick a topic that is about to be studied, and on a piece of paper list words and phrases that are connected to it. (2) Have students work with a partner or in groups to cut the words and phrases apart to use as manipulatives. (3) Have students discuss the words and concepts and put them into categories that are labeled by the group. (4) Have students make predictions as to what the topic will be about based on the concepts and categories. (5) Then, have students read the passage or chapter and then revisit the categories. (6) If necessary, have students re-sort the categories based on what they have read. (7) Have student groups create a final sort and provide a reason for why they sorted the categories as they did (Perez, 2008).

## REFLECTION AND APPLICATION

> **How will I incorporate *manipulatives, experiments, labs, and models* into instruction to engage students' brains?**

**Which manipulatives, experiments, labs, and models am I already integrating as I teach the curriculum?**

**What additional activities will I integrate?**

Strategy 8

# Metaphors, Analogies, and Similes

## WHAT: DEFINING THE STRATEGY

I was teaching the story *When Charlie McButton Lost Power* to a third-grade class in Mesquite, Texas. The curricular objective was for students to recognize the main idea and supporting details in narrative text. I used a simile as an instructional tool. I told the students that a main idea and details are like a table and legs. Just like the legs hold up the table, so do the details support the main idea. We drew a table with four legs on the dry-erase board. We concluded that the main idea from the story was that *Charlie was upset when he lost power.* I wrote that on the top of the table. Then I had students go back to the text and find evidence that Charlie was upset. One student found the place in the story where it said that, *He shrieked!* He came to the front of the room and wrote those words on one leg of our table. By the way, the lesson presented a wonderful opportunity for role play. Since some students didn't know what *shrieked* meant, I demonstrated and then we all *shrieked* together. That was fun! Students then found three additional examples from the text of the main idea, and we wrote one on each of the three remaining legs of our table. Because third-graders understood the concept of a table and legs, they now also understood the concept of a main idea and details.

Middle and high school students are best taught main idea by comparing the concept to Twitter. Since Twitter limits the number of characters, it would behoove the writer of a Tweet to limit the text to the most crucial or main ideas in the message. Students could even write the main idea of a story or expository text as if they are sending a Tweet.

81

Of all 20 strategies, this one is probably one of the most effective. Because the brain is a *maker of meaning*, it is constantly searching for connections and patterns. Students can understand many new and complicated concepts when those concepts are compared to dissimilar ones that the students already know and understand.

## WHY: THEORETICAL FRAMEWORK

"The hardware for making metaphors may be in-born, the software is earned and learned through living" (Popova, 2015).

Students would probably learn better if teachers used *metaphorical truth*, which is communicated by comparing two things but whose meaning goes beyond what is communicated by the actual words of the metaphor (Scott & Marzano, 2014, p. 90).

Metaphors, in general, elicit emotional responses from the brain, which provide a rhetorical advantage when people communicate with one another (Kelly, 2014).

When teachers use metaphorical connections to extend the thinking of students, the likelihood that students will understand the concept and remember it in the future is increased (Gregory & Chapman, 2013).

While metaphors convey meaning of content and skills as rapidly as literal language, they are customarily more rich in imagery (Sousa, 2011).

Analogies are very effective ways of getting students to conceptualize by comparing the similarities and differences in two pieces of information (Willis, 2006).

The effective use of humor, analogy, and metaphor in the college classroom can all contribute to increased comprehension, retention, and a more conducive learning environment (Garner, 2005).

When students use metaphor and analogy, two *semantic transformations*, to explain a concept, content becomes more coherent (Jensen, 2009a, p. 56).

Metaphor uses the familiar to explain something unfamiliar and describes the conceptual using something tangible (Jones, 2008).

When students connect what they are learning in mathematics with other content areas, math is viewed as more useful and interesting than when math is taught as a separate subject (Posamentier & Jaye, 2006).

Creating metaphors and creating analogies are two of the four types of tasks students should use to identify similarities and help them develop knowledge (Marzano, 2007).

Teachers who give students analogies when providing explanations have students who are capable of conceptualizing complex ideas (Posamentier & Jaye, 2006).

# HOW: INSTRUCTIONAL ACTIVITIES

**WHO:**            Elementary
**WHEN:**           During a lesson
**CONTENT AREA(S):**  Cross-curricular

• To introduce the concept of *simile*, read aloud the book *I'm as Quick as a Cricket* by Audrey Wood. Read it the first few times simply for enjoyment. Then have students think of ways they are like animals. Help them write a story using the following pattern: *I'm as _____ as a _____.* Compile their stories into a class book.

**WHO:**            Elementary
**WHEN:**           During a lesson
**CONTENT AREA(S):**  Mathematics

• Assist students in understanding that certain operations in math are analogous to other operations. Help them to see that addition and subtraction are simply inverse operations, as are multiplication and division. Show them that multiplication is simply a faster form of addition. Because the brain is constantly searching for connections, consistently demonstrating these relationships to students should help them to better understand and apply these concepts.

**WHO:**            Elementary/Middle/High
**WHEN:**           During a lesson
**CONTENT AREA(S):**  Cross-curricular

• Regardless of the content area, students should engage in Glynn's TWA (teaching with analogies) approach by using the following procedure:

   o Introduce the concept to be learned.
   o Review a familiar but similar concept through the use of analogy.
   o Identify the features of both the new and known concepts.
   o Explain what both concepts have in common.
   o Explain how the new concept is different from the known. (At this point the analogy breaks down.)
   o Draw conclusions regarding the major ideas that students need to remember about the new concept (Glynn, 1996).

**WHO:**            Elementary/Middle/High
**WHEN:**           During a lesson
**CONTENT AREA(S):**  Language arts

• Select a theme, such as *prejudice* or *growing up*, and have students compare and contrast several different stories, examining their approach to the particular theme. Have students cite text evidence that shows the similarities and differences in the treatment of the themes in two or more texts.

| | |
|---|---|
| **WHO:** | Elementary/Middle/High |
| **WHEN:** | During a lesson |
| **CONTENT AREA(S):** | Cross-curricular |

• Whenever possible, introduce a new or difficult concept by comparing it to a concept that students already know and understand, particularly one they will experience in the real world. For example, when teaching math students the meaning of logarithms, remind them that the Richter Scale for measuring the intensity of earthquakes is a logarithmic scale. When teaching the layers of the earth's sediment, have students compare those layers to the dirty clothing deposited in a laundry basket. The most recent deposits would be on the top in both instances.

| | |
|---|---|
| **WHO:** | Elementary/Middle/High |
| **WHEN:** | During a lesson |
| **CONTENT AREA(S):** | Cross-curricular |

• To assist students in comprehending the relationship between two concepts in any content area, have them create analogies. Give them the pattern a : b :: c : d (a is to b as c is to d) to show how two sets of ideas or concepts are related. For example, Shakespeare : *Hamlet* :: Charles Dickens : *A Christmas Carol* or Eli Whitney : the cotton gin :: Thomas Edison : the light bulb. Once they get the hang of it, students can then create their own analogies, leaving a blank line for other students to complete.

| | |
|---|---|
| **WHO:** | Elementary/Middle/High |
| **WHEN:** | After a lesson |
| **CONTENT AREA(S):** | Music |

• Assist students in seeing the analogous relationship between types of notes in music and fractions in math. For example, in 4/4 time, it takes two half notes, four quarter notes, and eight eighth notes to make a whole note. Similarly, it takes, 2/2, 4/4, and 8/8 to also make a whole. Have students write musical notation to symbolize fractional parts.

| | |
|---|---|
| **WHO:** | Elementary/Middle/High |
| **WHEN:** | During or after a lesson |
| **CONTENT AREA(S):** | Cross-curricular |

• Have students pretend to be detectives and look for metaphors, analogies, and similes in narrative and expository texts. Post a list of the examples students find, and periodically, ask students to explain the relationships that exist between the two concepts. Add to the list throughout the year.

| | |
|---|---|
| **WHO:** | Elementary/Middle/High |
| **WHEN:** | During a lesson |
| **CONTENT AREA(S):** | Language arts |

• As students write, have them create metaphors that improve the quality of their writing and symbolize their understanding of the relationship between two unrelated concepts. Have them explain the relationship to a partner. For example, students could write the following: *My life is a roller coaster. I have my ups and downs.*

**WHO:**                 Elementary/Middle/High
**WHEN:**                During a lesson
**CONTENT AREA(S):**     Cross-curricular

• To encourage creative thinking, have students complete a cloze sentence such as the following: If ____ were a ____, it would be ____ because ____. For example, *If the brain were a piece of technology, it would be a computer because it has a great deal of memory.*

**WHO:**                 Elementary/Middle/High
**WHEN:**                During a lesson
**CONTENT AREA(S):**     Social studies

• To understand that history repeats itself, help students connect current events to similar events that happened in the past. For example, students could compare the current recession with the Great Depression that occurred years earlier. Have them use a Venn diagram to compare and contrast how the two periods are alike and how they are different. Consult Strategy 5 for a model of a Venn diagram.

## REFLECTION AND APPLICATION

How will I incorporate *metaphors, analogies, and similes* into instruction to engage students' brains?

**Which metaphors, analogies, and similes am I already integrating as I teach the curriculum?**

**What additional activities will I integrate?**

# Strategy 9

# Mnemonic Devices

## WHAT: DEFINING THE STRATEGY

*IVAN CAPP:* Interjection, Verb, Adjective, Noun, Conjunction, Adverb, Pronoun, Preposition (Language arts)

*PEMDAS:* Please Excuse My Dear Aunt Sally (Math)

*HONC* if you're alive! Hydrogen, Oxygen, Nitrogen, Carbon (Science)

*HOMES:* Huron, Ontario, Michigan, Erie, Superior (Social studies)

*Every Good Boy Does Fine:* EGBDF (Music)

Mnemonic devices are acronyms and acrostics and can be found in every content area, as evidenced above. Acronyms are words where the first letter in the word stands for the content to be remembered. For example, *IVAN CAPP* helps students remember the eight parts of speech; *HOMES*, the Great Lakes; and *HONC*, the four atoms most important to life. Acrostics, on the other hand, are sentences where the first letter in each word in the sentence begins with the same letter as the concept to be remembered. For example, <u>P</u>lease <u>E</u>xcuse <u>M</u>y <u>D</u>ear <u>A</u>unt <u>S</u>ally actually helps students remember the order of operations in math (<u>P</u>arentheses, <u>E</u>xponents, <u>M</u>ultiply, <u>D</u>ivide, <u>A</u>dd, <u>S</u>ubtract). <u>E</u>very <u>G</u>ood <u>B</u>oy <u>D</u>oes <u>F</u>ine actually represents the notes on the lines of the treble clef, *EGBDF.*

Mnemonic devices serve as effective tools for remembering large amounts of information. In fact, the word itself derives from the Greek word *mnema*, which means memory. Mnemonic devices used in the real world to help the public remember include *acquired immune deficiency syndrome (AIDS),* or *sudden infant death syndrome (SIDS)* and one of the most widely used mnemonic devices today is *lol*, for *laughing out loud*.

## WHY: THEORETICAL FRAMEWORK

Acronyms and acrostics are two powerful techniques human beings can use to memorize information (Allen & Scozzi, 2012).

*Mnemonics*, derived from the Greek words *to remember*, are useful ways for remembering unrelated information, rules, or patterns (Sousa, 2011).

Adolescents find mnemonic devices more meaningful when they can personally create them (Feinstein, 2009).

Since students' brains have difficulty holding information that is not meaningful or does not have a *hook*, acrostics and acronyms help to provide that hook (Sprenger, 2008).

Learning is increased two- to three-fold when people rely on mnemonic devices rather than their regular learning habits (Markowitz & Jensen, 2007).

Mnemonic devices should be used only after students have had an opportunity to thoroughly process the information, even if their understanding is incomplete (Marzano, 2007).

An acronym turns a recall task into an *aided recall task* because students are remembering chunks of information rather than a lot of information at one time (Allen, 2008, p. 16).

Process mnemonics, such as PEMDAS (**P**lease **E**xcuse **M**y **D**ear **A**unt **S**ally), are very effective for students having difficulty in math because they are attention-getting, motivational, and actively engage the brain in processes essential to learning and memory (Sousa, 2007).

Retention and recall are improved when students are provided with a mnemonic aid (Ronis, 2006).

Regular people can greatly increase memory performance with mnemonic devices because they can be useful for recalling unrelated information, rules, or patterns (Sousa, 2006).

Mathematics instruction is more relevant and cohesive when mnemonics are used to link abstract symbols with concrete associations (Bender, 2005).

## HOW: INSTRUCTIONAL ACTIVITIES

**WHO:**              Elementary/Middle/High
**WHEN:**             During a lesson
**CONTENT AREA(S):**  Cross-curricular

• To assist students in recalling content previously taught and thoroughly processed, create acronyms and acrostics that will help them remember. Teach these mnemonic devices, and use them consistently during instruction so students hear them multiple times and can use them to recall content during and after tests. For example, to remember the five states that border Virginia, a social studies teacher could give students the acrostic *Kiss Me With No Teeth! Which stands for Kentucky, Maryland, West Virginia, North Carolina, and Tennessee* (Tate, 2012).

| | |
|---|---|
| **WHO:** | Elementary/Middle/High |
| **WHEN:** | During a lesson |
| **CONTENT AREA(S):** | Cross-curricular |

• Have students create their own acrostics to assist them in remembering content. For example, one teacher had students create original acrostics to remember the order of operations in math. Students will remember best what they choose to create themselves, especially if the mnemonic devices are humorous or novel. For example, instead of the customary *Please Excuse My Dear Aunt Sally* (**P**arentheses, **E**xponents, **M**ultiply, **D**ivide, **A**dd, **S**ubtract) one student created the following original acrostic: *Please End My Day At School.*

| | |
|---|---|
| **WHO:** | Elementary/Middle/High |
| **WHEN:** | During a lesson |
| **CONTENT AREA(S):** | Mathematics |

• To help eliminate the threat that occurs in the brain when some students lack confidence in their ability to be successful in your math class, teach them the acronym that Connie Moore of Los Angeles California uses: MATH, which actually stands for **M**ath **A**in't **T**hat **H**ard! I know that the word "ain't" is not grammatically correct, but this acronym is too good to overlook. If you use the 20 strategies as you teach, you can watch this acronym come true.

| | |
|---|---|
| **WHO:** | Elementary/Middle/High |
| **WHEN:** | During a lesson |
| **CONTENT AREA(S):** | Science |

• Have students remember the acrostic, *Never Does Eating Some Chocolate-Covered Goodies Really Ruin Meals,* to recall the 10 systems of the human body (in no particular order). They are **n**ervous, **d**igestive, **e**xcretory, **s**keletal, **c**irculatory, **c**overing, **g**land, **r**espiratory, **r**eproductive, and **m**uscular (Tate & Phillips, 2011). Medical doctors in my workshops have told me that the use of mnemonic devices to remember parts of the human body aided them in getting through medical school.

| | |
|---|---|
| **WHO:** | Elementary/Middle/High |
| **WHEN:** | During a lesson |
| **CONTENT AREA(S):** | Cross-curricular |

• Have students use the *Acrostics Topics* activity to recall important information regarding a topic being studied. Divide students into groups of four to six. Give each group a large piece of chart paper with a topic written horizontally down the left-hand side. This topic becomes an acronym that each group will use to list facts about the topic. The following example could be used in a social studies classroom:

C     Came to America for religious freedom
O     On long trips in boats
L     Loyalists agreed with the British King.
O     Often people farmed and hunted.
N     No taxation without representation
I     If you wanted independence, you were a patriot.
E     Even kids helped out with chores, such as cooking or fishing.
S     Some took the Native Americans' land.

Ask groups to share their finished products with the class. If groups cannot come up with a fact that begins with the designated letter, have them use information in their textbooks or from the Internet. Watch the creativity of your students blossom (Green & Casale-Giannola, 2011)!

**WHO:**              Elementary/Middle/High
**WHEN:**             During a lesson
**CONTENT AREA(S):**  Language arts

• Writing to convey information and writing to argue or persuade readers are the two types of writing required for incoming college students (ACT, 2009). The acronym *DEFENDS* provides students with a structure for finishing initial and final drafts of argumentative writing:

*Decide* on a specific position.
*Examine* own reasons for this position.
*Form* list of points explaining each reason.
*Expose* position in first sentence of written task.
*Note* each reason and associated points.
*Drive* home position in last sentence.
*Search* for and correct any errors (Collier, 2010, p. 207).

**WHO:**              Elementary/Middle/High
**WHEN:**             During a lesson
**CONTENT AREA(S):**  Cross-curricular

• Mnemonic devices are used in the real world consistently to help the public remember content that would be otherwise difficult to recall. Have students look for examples of mnemonic devices in the real world, such as SCUBA, CIA, or FBI, and bring their list to class. Post a list of real-life examples and see how many the class can come up with in a combined list.

**WHO:**              Elementary/Middle/High
**WHEN:**             During a lesson
**CONTENT AREA(S):**  Mathematics

• To help students comprehend the text of a word problem, use the *SQRQCQ* strategy, which serves as a mnemonic device:

**Survey:**　　　　　　Obtain a general understanding of the problem by reading it quickly.

**Question:**　　　　　Find out what information is required in the problem.

**Read:**　　　　　　Read the problem again to find information that is relevant to solving the problem.

**Question:**　　　　　Ask what operations must be performed and in which order to solve the problem.

**Complete:**　　　　　Do the computations necessary to get a solution.

**Question:**　　　　　Ask whether the answer is reasonable and the process complete.

**WHO:**　　　　　　　　Elementary/Middle/High
**WHEN:**　　　　　　　During a lesson
**CONTENT AREA(S):**　Mathematics, Science

• Have students remember the following acrostic to help them recall the prefixes for units of the metric system, from large to small: *Kids Have Dropped Over Dead Converting Metrics* which stands for kilo, hecto, deka, ones unit, deci, centi, milli.

**WHO:**　　　　　　　　High
**WHEN:**　　　　　　　During a lesson
**CONTENT AREA(S):**　Mathematics

• Have students remember the acrostic, *Some Old Hen Caught Another Hen Taking Oats Away*, to help them remember the following formulas:

$$\text{Sine} = \frac{\text{Opposite}}{\text{Hypotenuse}}$$

$$\text{Cosine} = \frac{\text{Adjacent}}{\text{Hypotenuse}}$$

$$\text{Tangent} = \frac{\text{Opposite}}{\text{Adjacent}}$$

Another high school teacher told me that he uses a similar acrostic, but his is as follows: *Some Old Hippie Caught Another Hippie Tripping On Acid.*

## REFLECTION AND APPLICATION

How will I incorporate *mnemonic devices* into instruction to engage students' brains?

**Which mnemonic devices am I already integrating as I teach the curriculum?**

**What additional devices will I integrate?**

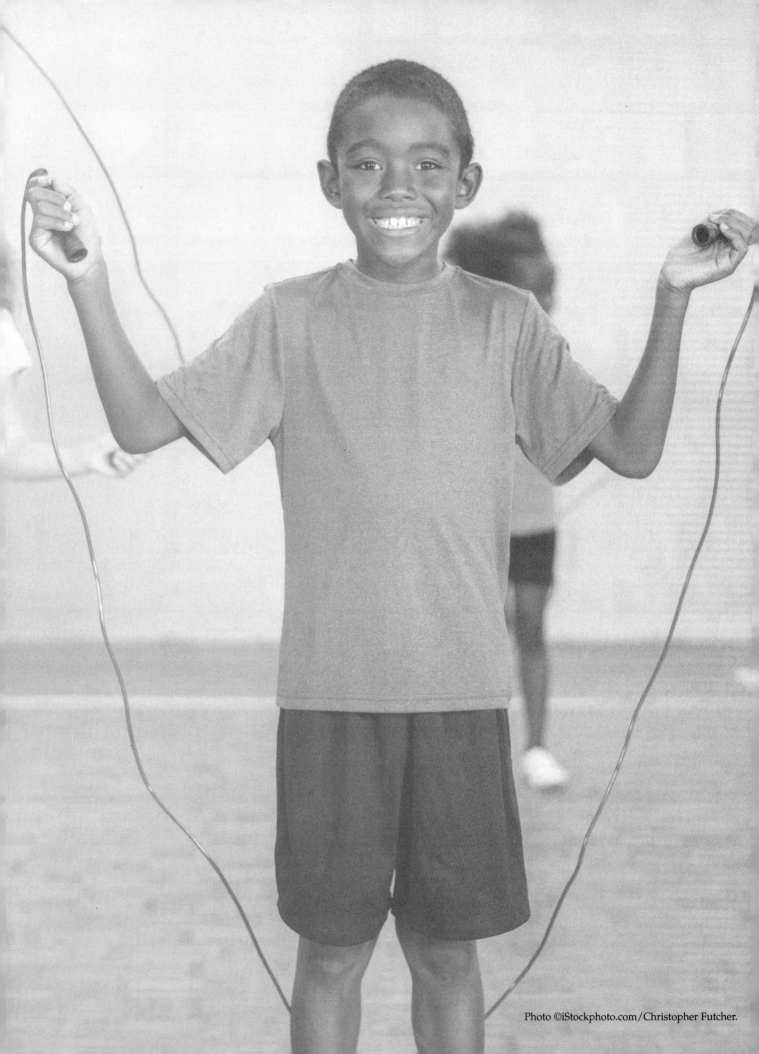

# Strategy 10

# Movement

## WHAT: DEFINING THE STRATEGY

Recently, I taught a lesson to fifth-graders where they were required to put the events in an expository text story called *The Snake* in sequential order. To integrate movement into the lesson, I took the major story events and put them on separate pieces of paper. Once we had read the story, I passed the papers out randomly to students and had them come to the front of the room holding their papers so that the rest of the class could read what was written on them. Then another student volunteered to come forward and move his classmates around until the events were in the order as they appeared in the story. By the way, to add a little fun, the task had to be completed before the theme from *The Price Is Right* ended. The remainder of the class had to decide whether the events were correctly ordered or not. Therefore, an interesting whole-class discussion ensued.

When students move while learning, they put information in *procedural* or *muscle* memory. Procedural memory is one of the strongest memory systems in the brain and the reason that one seldom forgets how to drive a car, ride a bicycle, play the piano, type on a keyboard, tie one's shoes, or brush one's teeth. One teacher related to me that her mother has Alzheimer's disease and no longer recognizes her or her children. She stated, however, that her mother still remembers how to play the piano and can still play songs that she always has!

In many traditional classrooms, students sit for long periods in uncomfortable desks, and if they get up, they are chastised for being out of their seats. One teacher commented to me that we spend the first three years of our children's lives teaching them to walk and talk and the next 15 telling them to *Sit down!* and *Shut up!* Rather than having students watching you as you move around the classroom, have them up and moving along with you. Not only does it strengthen memory and decrease behavior problems, but it also makes teaching and learning so much fun!

# WHY: THEORETICAL FRAMEWORK

The majority of the cerebellum and a part of the cerebrum are devoted to initiating and coordinating all types of movements that the body has previously learned (Sousa & Pilecki, 2013).

When students get up and move, they recirculate the blood that pools in their seats and feet when sitting for more than 20 minutes. Fifteen percent of this recirculated blood goes to the brain within a minute (Sousa, 2011).

Physical performance is probably the only known cognitive activity that uses 100 percent of the brain (Jensen, 2008).

Higher concentrations of oxygen in the blood caused by physical activity enabled young adults to increase the speed at which they performed visual and spatial tasks and recalled more words (Chung et al., 2009).

The same parts of the brain (the cerebellum, motor cortex, and mid-brain) that coordinate movement also coordinate the flow of thoughts, resulting in complex problems often being solved just by taking a walk (Sousa, 2011).

Regular exercise increases the levels of brain-derived neurotrophic factor (BDNF), which keeps existing neurons healthy, helps them communicate with neighboring neurons, and facilitates the growth of new neurons (Sousa, 2012).

Dance is not only a form of communication, but it also improves attention to detail and can assist students with sequencing and thinking logically (Karten, 2009).

Having students work quietly at their desks eliminates up to 40 percent of kinesthetic learners who have to be moving to learn (Hattie, 2009).

Movement triggers memory because the basal ganglia and cerebellum, once thought to be only associated with controlling muscle movement, have been found to be important in coordinating thought processes as well (Markowitz & Jensen, 2007).

Because physical movement increases the energy of students, it, therefore, enhances their engagement (Marzano, 2007).

Movement not only assists with reading, gets blood and glucose to the brain, changes the state or mood of the brain, and provides lots of fun during learning, but it also assists with our strongest memory system—procedural memory (Sprenger, 2007b).

Instructional situations that involve the use of movement necessitate more sensory input than do situations requiring only paper and pencil (Gregory & Parry, 2006).

Repeat a movement often enough and that movement becomes a permanent memory (Sprenger, 2007a).

# HOW: INSTRUCTIONAL ACTIVITIES

**WHO:**　　　　　　　　　　Elementary/Middle/High
**WHEN:**　　　　　　　　　Before a lesson
**CONTENT AREA(S):**　　Cross-curricular

• Have students draw the *appointment clock* on their paper. Put on fast-paced music and have students move around the classroom making appointments with four students in class, one appointment for 12 o'clock, a different student for 3 o'clock, a different one for 6 o'clock, and a final student for 9 o'clock. Have them write each student's name on the corresponding line. Then, as you teach lessons throughout the day or week, have students keep their appointments by discussing content with one another or re-teaching a concept previously taught.

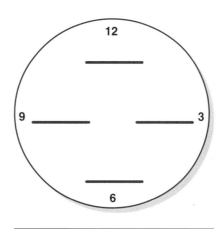

**Adaptation:** Students can also make appointments using the following: A seasonal appointment clock, a timeline in social studies, or quadrants in mathematics.

**Figure 10.1**

**Seasonal Dates**

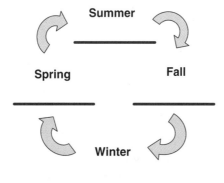

**Figure 10.2**

# Appointment Timeline

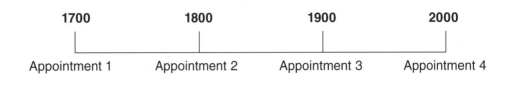

| 1700 | 1800 | 1900 | 2000 |
|------|------|------|------|

Appointment 1    Appointment 2    Appointment 3    Appointment 4

_____    _____    _____    _____

## Quadrant Appointments

| Quadrant 2 <br> _____ | Quadrant 1 <br> _____ |
|---|---|
| Quadrant 3 <br> _____ | Quadrant 4 <br> _____ |

**Figure 10.3**

| | |
|---|---|
| **WHO:** | Elementary |
| **WHEN:** | During a lesson |
| **CONTENT AREA(S):** | Mathematics |

• Have the entire class skip-count aloud by 2s, 3s, 5s, 10s, 20s, and so on. Add movement by having them clap or take turns jumping rope while skip counting.

| | |
|---|---|
| **WHO:** | Elementary/Middle/High |
| **WHEN:** | During a lesson |
| **CONTENT AREA(S):** | Cross-curricular |

• Rather than having students always raise their hand if they agree with an answer provided by a classmate, have them stand if they agree and remain seated if they disagree. Standing provides more blood and oxygen throughout the body and keeps students more alert.

**WHO:**                    Elementary/Middle/High
**WHEN:**                   During a lesson
**CONTENT AREA(S):**        Cross-curricular

• When discussing content with their families (or students seated near them) for one or two minutes, have students stand and talk rather than remain seated.

**WHO:**                    Elementary/Middle/High
**WHEN:**                   During a lesson
**CONTENT AREA(S):**        Cross-curricular

• Have students take turns standing and reading short passages aloud in a choral response. Because students are reading together, those students who may be struggling can still participate and will hear the passage read correctly by others. Make this activity more fun by having students read while standing on one foot, in a whisper, holding their paper in the air, without taking a breath, and so forth.

**WHO:**                    Elementary/Middle
**WHEN:**                   During a lesson
**CONTENT AREA(S):**        Language arts

• To help students distinguish between common and proper nouns, use the following activity. Compile a list containing both common and proper nouns taken from content previously taught in class. Read each word aloud. Have students stand when a proper noun is called, since proper nouns are extremely important, and remain seated when a common noun is called, since common nouns are not as important.

**WHO:**                    Elementary/Middle/High
**WHEN:**                   During a lesson
**CONTENT AREA(S):**        Music

• Have students sit in chairs that represent the lines (EGBDF) on the treble clef. Other students stand in spaces between the chairs and represent the spaces (FACE) on the treble clef. When a note is called out or played on an instrument, have students stand if seated or squat, if standing, if their position on the scale corresponds to the note played. Once they are familiar with the treble clef notes, engage them in the same activity using the lines and spaces on the bass clef.

**WHO:**                    Elementary/Middle/High
**WHEN:**                   During the lesson
**CONTENT AREA(S):**        Mathematics

• Engage students in the *circumference conga* to teach students the concepts of *circumference, radius,* and *diameter*. Have all students in class form a circle. Stand in the middle of the circle. Have them do the conga by putting their hands on the shoulders of the person in front of them and moving to the salsa music. The circle represents the *circumference*. When you say, "Turn," have them reverse the circle. Then say, "Freeze" and the circle stops. Then point to a student in the circle and appoint them as the *radius.* The radius then dances (or walks) over to you and then back to their original position (because the radius only extends to the center of the circle). The circle (circumference) then moves again. Say, "Freeze." Then point to a different student in the circle who can be the *diameter*. The diameter dances (walks) over to you and then straight to the opposite side (because the diameter goes all the way through the circle). Repeat this dance for as long as you desire. Gloria Estefan's song "Conga" is the perfect music for this activity.

| | |
|---|---|
| **WHO:** | Elementary/Middle/High |
| **WHEN:** | During a lesson |
| **CONTENT AREA(S):** | Cross-curricular |

• When teaching sequential order (such as events in history, action in a story, or steps in the scientific process), put the separate events or steps on pieces of paper and then pass them out to students in class. Put on fast-paced music, such as the theme from *The Price Is Right*, and have students place themselves in sequential order before the music ends. Then have the class decide if students have placed themselves correctly.

| | |
|---|---|
| **WHO:** | Middle/High |
| **WHEN:** | During a lesson |
| **CONTENT AREA(S):** | Mathematics |

• Have students do the "Number Line Hustle." Draw a number line on the board. Explain the position of the positive and negative integers on the number line. Have students stand and tell them that they will be doing the "Number Line Hustle" by moving along the number line. Have each student stand in a place in the room where they have space to move to the left and to the right. They should all be facing in the same direction, turned toward the number line on the board. You may use any appropriate disco music, such as Van McCoy's *The Hustle*. Put on the music and then position yourself in front of the class. Lead the class in the movements necessary to solve the following problems:

(Problem I: +5 + −3 = ?) Have students move with you to the music five steps in a positive direction (+5). Then have them move three steps in a negative direction (−3). Ask them what number they landed on. The class should say +2.

Ask the class what they would have to do to get back to zero. (They should say move two steps in a negative direction.) Have them move back to zero.

(Problem II: −6 + +10 = ?) Starting at zero, have students move six steps in a negative direction (−6). Then have them move +10 steps in a positive direction. Ask the class, "What number are you on?" (+4)

Have the class sit down. Put the same problems that you danced out on the board so that students can see the connection between the concrete and the abstract. Then provide five additional problems for students to work either individually or in pairs. Give students the option of going to the back of the classroom and dancing along the number line to solve the additional problems while the music continues to play softly in the background. I have actually taught students this lesson three times and it works every time.

# REFLECTION AND APPLICATION

How will I incorporate *movement* into
instruction to engage students' brains?

**Which movement activities am I already integrating as I teach the
curriculum?**

**What additional activities will I integrate?**

# Strategy 11

# Music, Rhythm, Rhyme, and Rap

## WHAT: DEFINING THE STRATEGY

When I teach model lessons to K–12 students, I always play classical music before the lesson begins. If I am teaching elementary students, I go to each desk and introduce myself while they are listening to the music. If the students are in middle or high school, I am at the door to greet them as they change classes. You would be surprised at the number of students who do not know how to look me in the eye, give me a hearty handshake, and offer a warm greeting. Maybe you wouldn't be surprised! It appears to me that we are allowing technology to supersede our ability to engage in face-to-face social interaction. But, I digress!

"His music teacher says he has van Gogh's ear for music."

SOURCE: Bacall (2003a).

Before I begin the lesson, I ask students if they know what type of music I am playing and how it makes them feel. At least one student inevitably recognizes the type of music, and I have received comments such as *It relaxes me! It calms me down! It makes me sleepy! I like it! It sounds strange!* What I am attempting to do is get students' brains in a state of relaxed alertness so that they will do well on the subsequent lesson. And they do!

Two other uses of music have to do with its effect on memory and its relationship to mathematical ability. Whenever students put content to music, they stand a better chance of remembering it. Some research (Jensen, 2007; Wiley-Blackwell, 2009) also suggests that the same spatial part of the brain that is activated when one is playing a musical instrument or sight-reading music is also activated when one is solving higher-level math problems. In a study by Catterall, Chapleau, and Iwanga (1999), the mathematics scores of low socioeconomic students more than doubled for those who took music lessons compared to those who did not. My daughter Jessica, who took more than 10 years of piano lessons, played in the band, and sung in the chorus in high school and college, did very well on the math section of the SAT.

## WHY: THEORETICAL FRAMEWORK

There are certain structures in the auditory cortex of the brain that respond only to the tones of music (Sousa & Pilecki, 2013).

Pop music can increase concentration and raise endorphin levels while Baroque music can calm and soothe (Gregory & Chapman, 2013).

As a mood enhancer, music can calm or cheer stressed or grumpy students and motivate those who are reluctant (Allen & Scozzi, 2012).

Music has the remarkable ability to energize, relax, set the daily mood, stimulate student brains, inspire, and make the learning fun (Jensen, 2009a).

Since music can act as a volume barrier, playing it while students are collaborating can keep the noise level low (Allen & Currie, 2012).

Music activates neural networks in the brain, which stimulate both the intellect and the emotion (Sousa, 2011).

Music can be used as a signal, when students are moving, to match a theme, during small-group discussions, or after class (Allen & Scozzi, 2012).

When given tests of visual, phonological, and executive memory, people who were musicians outperformed people who were not (George & Coch, 2011).

When one listens to background music, attention, concentration recall of information, visual imagery, and dexterity are enhanced (Sousa, 2011).

Music that makes one feel good should not be played during direct instruction or as background music when students are writing, reading, or during group or project-based instruction (Allen & Wood, 2013).

Music lessons taken either in or out of school correlate positively with increased academic achievement in reading and math (Wiley-Blackwell, 2009).

The critical ingredient for improving the performance of students on spatial tasks is musical rhythm (Jensen, 2007).

Fast music with 100 to 140 beats per minute can be energizing for the brain, while calming music at 40 to 55 beats per minute can be relaxing (Jensen, 2005).

The rhythms, contrasts, and patterns of music help the brain encode new information, which is why students easily learn words to new songs (Jensen, 2005).

# HOW: INSTRUCTIONAL ACTIVITIES

**WHO:** Elementary/Middle/High
**WHEN:** Before, during, or after a lesson
**CONTENT AREA(S):** Cross-curricular

- A rule of thumb for your use of music in class is less than one-third of your class time. I never play music when I am doing direct instruction to my class. It can be very distracting to have music playing in the background when you want students to pay rapt attention to what you are saying. I might use music if students are writing creatively or solving math problems, but I would choose music without lyrics and I would keep the volume extremely low. I am even finding on an airplane that when music without lyrics is played prior to our departure, I can still simultaneously read my book. However, when music with lyrics is played, I have a difficult time focusing and paying attention.

**WHO:** Elementary/Middle/High
**WHEN:** Before or after a lesson
**CONTENT AREA(S):** Cross-curricular

- Appoint a disc jockey in each class whose job it is to play the music that you request when you request it. One student can fulfill that role for one week and at the end of the week, the responsibility shifts to another student who is interested in the job. Make playlists on your iPod or iPad for your disc jockey to make the job easier.

**WHO:** Elementary/Middle/High
**WHEN:** Before, during, or after a lesson
**CONTENT AREA(S):** Cross-curricular

- To maximize instructional time and minimize transition time, play music. Music with approximate beats of 50 to 70 per minute line up with the heart and calm the brain. This music can include classical, jazz, New Age, Celtic, Native American, or nature sounds. Have this type of music playing as students enter your room to help to ensure appropriate behavior for the beginning of class. Teach students that if you can hear their voices over the music, they are talking too loudly.

| | |
|---|---|
| **WHO:** | Elementary/Middle/High |
| **WHEN:** | Before, during, or after a lesson |
| **CONTENT AREA(S):** | Cross-curricular |

- Rather than calming music, oftentimes high-energy music is the order of the day. Music with beats of 110 to 160 per minute energizes the brain and body and can bring excitement to your lesson. This type of music can include salsa, rhythm and blues, rock and roll, positive rap, and fast-paced country. High-energy music is often needed for the afternoon classes when students have eaten lunch and appear to display the mnemonic device *TEGO* (*The Eyes Glaze Over!*).

| | |
|---|---|
| **WHO:** | Elementary/Middle/High |
| **WHEN:** | Before, during, or after a lesson |
| **CONTENT AREA(S):** | Cross-curricular |

- Review content with students using rock, rap, or country CDs from the company Rock 'N Learn. Each CD comes packaged with a DVD and book, and can be found at a local teacher store or by logging on to www .rocknlearn.com.

Google "rhythm, rhyme, and results" to gain access to educational rap and hip-hop songs for teaching across the curriculum.

Go to www.wphillips.com and look for *Sing Along Science* to access songs for teaching science concepts. The lyrics of these songs are written by Warren Phillips, former eighth-grade exemplary science teacher and 2004 Disney Middle School Teacher of the Year.

Here's something really great: Download the app *Songify* into your iPad or iPhone and then dictate your lyrics into *Songify*. They will take your lyrics and put them to a beat or to music for you.

| | |
|---|---|
| **WHO:** | Elementary/Middle/High |
| **WHEN:** | During a lesson |
| **CONTENT AREA(S):** | Cross-curricular |

- Find appropriate music to accompany your lesson and incorporate it directly into your teaching. For example, Billy Preston's *Will It Go Round in Circles* is perfect for teaching circumference in math, and Billy Joel's *We Didn't Start the Fire* can accentuate your history lesson.

| **WHO:** | Elementary/Middle/High |
|---|---|
| **WHEN:** | Before or after a lesson |
| **CONTENT AREA(S):** | Cross-curricular |

• If you do not want to go to the trouble of downloading your own music, consult the following websites for music appropriate to the classroom: www .di.fm, www.radiotunes.com, www.Live365.com, www.pandora.com, www .lastfm.com, and www.playlist.com.

| **WHO:** | Elementary/Middle/High |
|---|---|
| **WHEN:** | Before a lesson |
| **CONTENT AREA(S):** | Cross-curricular |

• Music can change the state of students' brains. Consult books that contain the research and can assist you with your selection of music. Two such books are *Top Tunes for Teaching* (1995) by Eric Jensen and *The Rock 'n' Roll Classroom: Using Music to Manage Mood, Energy, and Learning* (2013) by Rich Allen and W. W. Wood. Listed below are some of my personal favorite artists and selections that I use when teaching both students and adults.

## Calming Music for the Brain

*Classical Music*

- *The Most Relaxing Classical Album in the World*
- *The Most Relaxing Classical Album in the World—Ever!* (Disc 1)

*New Age Music*

- *The Most Relaxing New Age Music in the Universe*
- *Tribute to Enya*

*Piano Music—Emile Pandolfi*

- *An Affair to Remember*
- *By Request*
- *Days of Wine and Roses*
- *Secret Love*
- *Some Enchanted Evening*

*Jazz*

- *At Last . . . The Duet's Album* (Kenny G.)
- *The Ultimate Kenny G.*
- *Best of Hiroshima*
- *The Best Smooth Jazz Ever!* (Disc I)
- *Boney James*
- *The Greatest Hits of All* (George Benson)
- *Stardust . . . The Great American Songbook: Vol. III* (Rod Stewart)

## High-Energy Music for the Brain

*Artists' Greatest Hits*

- *Doobies*
- *Earth, Wind and Fire: Greatest Hits*
- *Greatest Hits* (Gloria Estefan)
- *Hits* (Phil Collins)
- *Song Review: A Greatest Hits Collection* (Stevie Wonder)
- *Sounds of Summer* (Beach Boys)
- *Suddenly '70s* (Greatest Hits of the 1970s)
- *The Hits* (Faith Hill)
- *The Very Best of Kool & the Gang*
- *The Very Best of Chic*
- *The Very Best of the Bee Gees*

*Artists' Single Hits for Motivating Students*

- "Ain't No Stopping Us Now!" (McFadden and Whitehead)
- "Best Day of My Life" (American Authors)
- "Celebration" (Kool & The Gang)
- "Don't Worry, Be Happy!" (Bobby McFerrin)
- "Eye of the Tiger" (Survivor)
- "Firework" (Katy Perry)
- "Girl on Fire" (Alicia Keys)
- "Happy" (Pharrell Williams)
- "Rather Be" (Clean Bandit)
- "Roar" (Katy Perry)
- "Shining Star" (Earth, Wind and Fire)
- "Rolling in the Deep" (Adele)
- "Skyfall" (Adele)
- "Something to Talk About" (Bonnie Raitt)
- "We Are the Champions" (Queen)
- "We Will Rock You" (Queen)
- "Stronger (What Doesn't Kill You)" (Kelly Clarkson)

| | |
|---|---|
| **WHO:** | Elementary/Middle/High |
| **WHEN:** | After a lesson |
| **CONTENT AREA(S):** | Cross-curricular |

- To assist students in recalling information following a lesson, have them walk, march, or dance around the room to high-energy, fast-paced music. Periodically, stop the music and have students form groups of three or four with other students standing in close proximity. Have them recall a major concept covered in the lesson and discuss it with their respective groups. Then start the music again and have them walk in a different direction so that when they stop, they are not standing next to the same students. Have them repeat the procedure with another group and another major concept.

**WHO:**                         Elementary/Middle/High
**WHEN:**                        Before a lesson
**CONTENT AREA(S):**             Cross-curricular

• Put your creative talents to work! Write an original song, rhyme, or rap to symbolize your understanding of a concept you have previously taught the class. Perform your creative effort for your students and teach it to them so that they can use the powerful effects of music to remember your content. They'll love you for it!

**WHO:**                         Elementary/Middle/High
**WHEN:**                        After a lesson
**CONTENT AREA(S):**             Cross-curricular

• Have students work in cooperative groups to write a cinquain that symbolizes their understanding of a concept previously taught or content read. The format of a cinquain is as follows: first line—one word, second line—two words, third line—three words, fourth line—four words, last line—one word.

## Example

*Brain*

*Social organism*

*Thinking, linking, connecting*

*Necessary for life itself*

*Life*

**WHO:**                         Elementary/Middle/High
**WHEN:**                        After a lesson
**CONTENT AREA(S):**             Cross-curricular

• Following instruction in a major concept, have students write an original song, rhyme, or rap to symbolize their understanding of the concept previously taught. Students can be assigned this task for homework, if class time does not permit. Then on the following day, all students in a social studies class, for example, can attend the *Talent Show*, where volunteers pretend to be on *American History Idol* rather than *American Idol* and get up and perform their original effort for the class. What a fun way to review content! By the way, when students are taking content and putting it into a different form, such as a song, rhyme, or rap, they are using one of the highest-level thinking skills available to them—synthesis.

## REFLECTION AND APPLICATION

How will I incorporate *music, rhythm, rhyme, and rap* into instruction to engage students' brains?

**Which music, rhythm, rhyme, and rap activities am I already integrating as I teach the curriculum?**

**What additional activites will I integrate?**

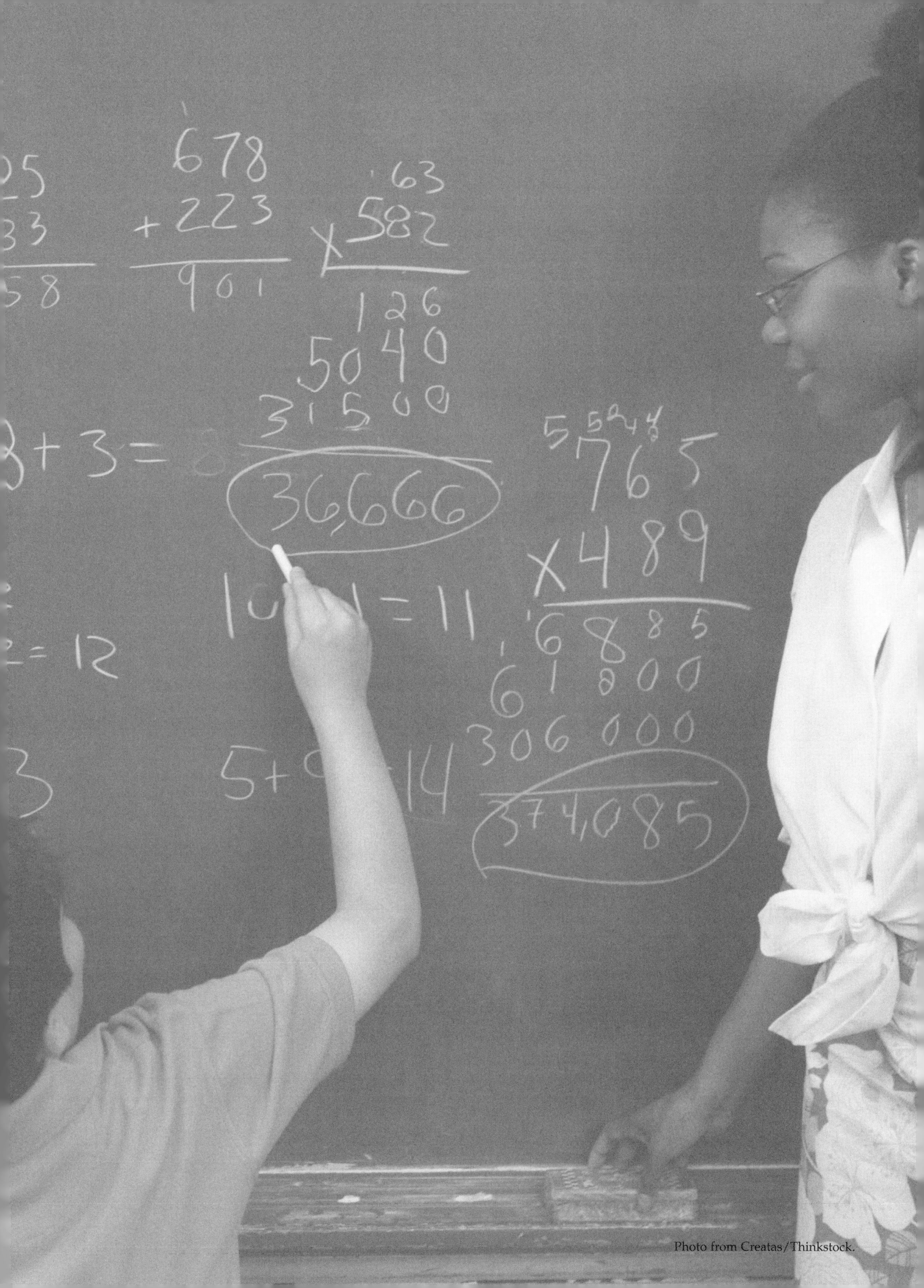


Photo from Creatas/Thinkstock.

Photo from Creatas/Thinkstock.

# Strategy 12

# Project-Based and Problem-Based Learning

## WHAT: DEFINING THE STRATEGY

When I teach math, if the objective involves problem solving, I never use the problems in the book as my initial examples. Most do not have any real meaning for students. Generic problems can be used for practice later, but students need to know how this skill appears in the real world. If they cannot see the correlation between what you are teaching in class

"I couldn't think of a science fair project so I just re-invented the wheel."

SOURCE: Bacall (2003a).

117

and their lives, they will often ask you *Why do we have to learn this?* Therefore, I try to figure out where this concept shows up in the world of the student, and I even integrate the names of some of the students into the problem.

Here's a specific example. I was teaching a class of eighth-grade special education students how to take a word problem and turn it into an algebraic equation. I began the lesson by asking the students if any one of them had been to a movie lately. One student, Camry, indicated that she had seen the movie, *Insidious: Chapter 2*. Although I have never seen that movie, I somehow did not think it was appropriate for an eighth-grader but since that was not the point of the lesson, I continued. I asked Camry how much she paid to get in, to which she replied $8.00. We visualized that there were two other students attending the movie and that Camry was paying for all three to which she commented, *I'm not about to do that!* At least, I had her attention! I asked Camry what snacks she purchased. She replied, *popcorn, Coke, and M&Ms.* We estimated the cost of the popcorn at $6.00, the coke at $4.00, and the *M&Ms* at $2.50. We then set up the following equation: x = 3($8.00) + $6.00 + $4.00 + $2.50.

Every student was motivated to find out exactly how much money Camry had spent, and I accomplished my goals, which were two-fold: (1) to demonstrate to students how to create and solve equations and (2) to show how this math concept can be applied in real life. That is what problem- and project-based learning do very well for the brain!

## WHY: THEORETICAL FRAMEWORK

Projects enable students to plan their time and develop research skills, while providing them with choice and responsibility (Gregory & Chapman, 2013).

Project-based learning is a 21st century approach that differentiates instruction while simultaneously encouraging high levels of student engagement (Bender, 2012).

When engaged in project-based learning, students are working at abstract and complex levels while still addressing their individual skill levels and rates of learning (Gregory & Chapman, 2013).

Two types of projects for student engagement are presentation projects (those that gather information and present it in a different way) and idea projects (those that focus on new ideas or take information and use it for a different purpose) (Delandtsheer, 2011).

When teachers are creating opportunities for students to observe, make inferences, and share their discoveries with peers, they are building the problem-solving skills advocated by the national standards for social studies (Melber & Hunter, 2010).

Problem-based learning "encompasses a rethinking of the entire curriculum so that teachers design whole units around complex, ill-structured problematic scenarios that embody the major concepts to be mastered and understood" (Barell, 2010, p. 178).

Problems stimulate brain activity as it seeks patterns, makes sense, finds connections, and functions effectively while bringing harmony to the dissonance it senses in the problem (Fogarty, 2009).

One of the highest correlations in a meta-analysis regarding the quality of teaching and student learning comes when teachers challenge students by encouraging them to think through and solve problems, either as a group or individually (Hattie, 2009).

"The more complex the problem, the more complex the brain activity becomes" (Fogarty, 2009, p. 167).

Problem solving to the brain is what aerobic exercise is to the body since solving challenging, complex problems creates a flourish of neural activity. Synapses form, blood flow increases, and neurotransmitters are activated (Jensen, 2008).

Teaching problem-solving strategies using the interest of students of all disabilities and grade levels keeps them involved and capitalizes on their natural inclination to solve meaningful problems in the context of real life (Algozzine, Campbell, & Wang, 2009b).

Educators should use such authentic tools as projects, discussions, and portfolios in addition to paper-and-pencil tests to demonstrate students' comprehension of mathematics (Ronis, 2006).

# HOW: INSTRUCTIONAL ACTIVITIES

**WHO:** Elementary/Middle/High
**WHEN:** During a lesson
**CONTENT AREA(S):** Mathematics

- When introducing a new concept in math class, create real-world problems incorporating the names of students in the class. As you solve the problem, talk out loud so that students can follow the thought processes involved. For example, when teaching the concept of elapsed time, have a student in class, let's say her name is Denise, share her typical daily schedule, such as what time she gets up, gets to school, arrives home, eats dinner, goes to bed, and so forth. Write the schedule on the board. Then, have students figure out how much time elapses from the time Denise does one thing to the time she does something else. Using the context of a student's real-world experiences makes the content more relevant and meaningful. After showing three or more examples where you model the thought processes, have students work individually, in pairs, or in small groups to solve additional problems.

**WHO:**                    Elementary/Middle/High
**WHEN:**                   During a lesson
**CONTENT AREA(S):**        Mathematics

- Have students work in groups and follow these steps when solving math problems:

    o Read the problem.
    o Comprehend the problem.
    o Analyze the problem.
    o Plan an approach that can be used to solve the problem.
    o Explore the approach to ascertain whether it will work.
    o Use the plan to solve the problem.
    o Verify the solution.
    o Listen to and observe other students while solving the problem (Posamentier & Jaye, 2006).

These steps could be put in a graphic organizer and placed as a visual on the wall for students to follow when solving math problems.

**WHO:**                    Elementary/Middle/High
**WHEN:**                   Before a lesson
**CONTENT AREA(S):**        Mathematics

- Have students create their own math problems for other students to solve. When students enter the room, have one student's problem on the board as a *sponge activity*. The problem could provide a review of a problem-solving strategy already taught and could supply some needed practice. Students could earn extra points by solving one another's problems correctly, either individually or with a partner.

**WHO:**                    Elementary/Middle/High
**WHEN:**                   During a lesson
**CONTENT AREA(S):**        Cross-curricular

- Identify multiple objectives from a number of content areas. Create a real-life project for students that will address all of the chosen objectives. For example, a project in which students write and produce a news program could address multiple objectives in a real-world, memorable context. Objectives for this project could include the following: researching major current or historical events to determine the stories to be included in the broadcast, writing news copy that is grammatically correct with a main idea sentence in each paragraph, or broadcasting the news using appropriate public speaking skills.

**WHO:**                    Elementary
**WHEN:**                   During a lesson
**CONTENT AREA(S):**        Mathematics

• Have students construct a class cookbook to apply their understanding of multiplying fractions. Have students find recipes for their favorite foods that have fractions of servings: for example, 2½ cups of flour, 2¼ cups of sugar, ¾ teaspoon of vanilla. Students then rewrite the recipe cutting it in half and then doubling and tripling it. Students can choose one version of the recipe to make as a project for homework.

**WHO:**               Elementary/Middle/High
**WHEN:**              After a lesson
**CONTENT AREA(S):**   Science

• To help them recall the parts of an animal cell, have students complete a project for a homework assignment. Have them make a pizza that displays their knowledge of the parts of the cell. Students will decide what toppings will be used to replicate parts of the cell, such as pepperoni for the nucleus or for the cytoplasm. On a designated day, have students bring their pizzas to school and evaluate one another's pizzas based on a rubric students helped to develop. Following the evaluation, be sure the class eats their pizzas and enjoys a "Cellabration!"

**WHO:**               Elementary/Middle/High
**WHEN:**              Before or during a lesson
**CONTENT AREA(S):**   Cross-curricular

• Have students use advanced searches to gather information from a variety of print and digital sources that could aid them in solving a problem or completing an assigned project. Students could evaluate the usefulness of each source in light of the problem or project and the audience. Have students integrate the information, without plagiarism, into the text so that they are not overly dependent on any one source (Tate, 2014a).

**WHO:**               Elementary/Middle/High
**WHEN:**              During a lesson
**CONTENT AREA(S):**   Science

• Have students create a timeline that shows a geologic history of life. One meter on the timeline could equal one million years. This scale will show the vast amount of time with no life on earth and the relative success of sustained life for the dinosaurs. Younger students could draw rather than write out timeline events (Tate & Phillips, 2011, p. 102).

**WHO:**               Middle/High
**WHEN:**              During a lesson
**CONTENT AREA(S):**   Cross-curricular

• Engage students in interdisciplinary cooperative learning projects such as the following. The class forms into student teams of four to six.

Each team selects one football, basketball, or baseball team to follow for 10 to 20 games of the regular season. Each team will choose the most valuable player of the team for the 10- to 20-week period, but they must be ready to justify the choice using vital statistics as evidence. The team will plan and deliver a broadcast including a PowerPoint presentation during which they will report analysis and interpretation of the stats. They will also submit journals in which they have tracked the team's statistics.

| | |
|---|---|
| **WHO:** | Middle/High |
| **WHEN:** | During or after a lesson |
| **CONTENT AREA(S):** | Mathematics |

- To assist students with the real-life skill of building a budget, have them work in cooperative groups. Give each group an allotted yearly income of, for example, $30,000. Have students plan a budget that allows for living expenditures such as housing, utilities, food, car payments, gas for car, car and health insurance, and so forth. Have students research the average cost of each expenditure and build a realistic annual budget. This project goes a long way toward helping students realistically understand just how much money it actually takes to live.

| | |
|---|---|
| **WHO:** | Elementary/Middle/High |
| **WHEN:** | During a lesson |
| **CONTENT AREA(S):** | Cross-curricular |

- Have students conduct short research projects for the purpose of answering a question. Have them draw research from multiple sources and generate additional related questions that call for them to explore additional print and digital sources for information.

| | |
|---|---|
| **WHO:** | Elementary/Middle/High |
| **WHEN:** | During a lesson |
| **CONTENT AREA(S):** | Cross-curricular |

- Place students in cooperative groups of four to six. Give each group a real-world problem to solve. Problems could include such topics as the following:

  - How would you increase parental participation in this school?
  - How would you decrease the unemployment rate in the country?
  - How can we increase the number of students taking advanced-placement classes in this school?

Have students collect and analyze data and work together to derive the best solution to the problem. Have each group write a paper outlining the problem and possible solution(s) and make an oral presentation to the class.

| | |
|---|---|
| **WHO:** | Elementary/Middle/High |
| **WHEN:** | During a lesson |
| **CONTENT AREA(S):** | Cross-curricular |

- When solving problems during class discussions, allow students to take turns sharing their ideas. Have them use sample sentence starters such as the following:

    o I realized that . . .
    o I agree with your thinking and would like to add . . .
    o I don't understand what you meant when you said . . .
    o I solved the problem this way . . .

| | |
|---|---|
| **WHO:** | Elementary/Middle/High |
| **WHEN:** | During the lesson |
| **CONTENT AREA(S):** | Cross-curricular |

- During a science or technical experiment, have students formulate a hypothesis. Have them collect data and use corroborating sources to verify the data. Have students then analyze the data to determine if they support or disprove the hypothesis. Have them draw conclusions and, if possible, use other sources of information to support those conclusions (Tate, 2014a).

## REFLECTION AND APPLICATION

How will I incorporate *project-based and problem-based learning* to engage students' brains?

Which project-based and problem-based learning activities am I already integrating as I teach the curriculum?

What additional activities will I integrate?

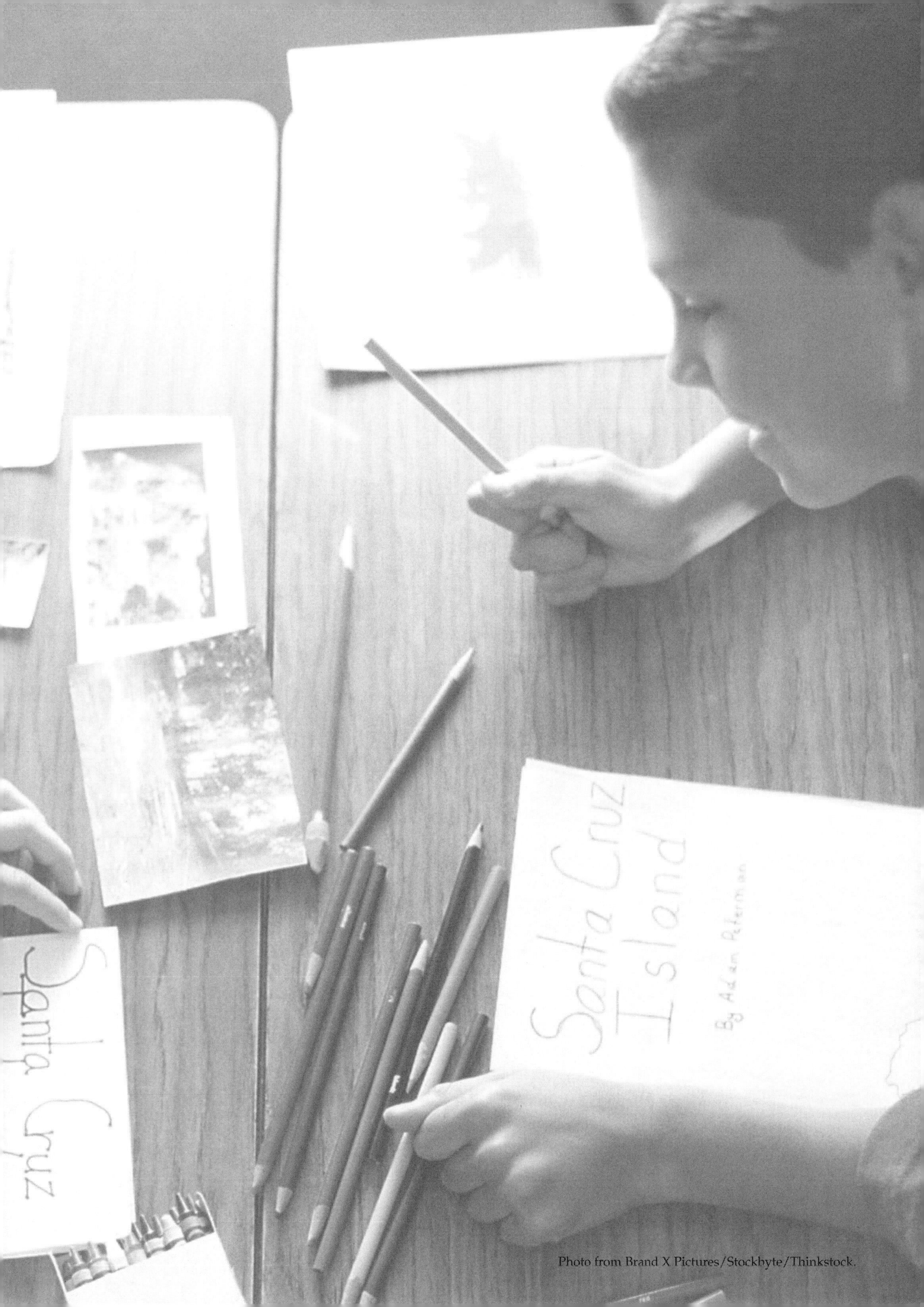


Photo from Brand X Pictures/Stockbyte/Thinkstock.

Strategy **13**

# Reciprocal Teaching and Cooperative Learning

## WHAT: DEFINING THE STRATEGY

When I was taught to teach more than 40 years ago, if two students were talking together about content, they were accused of cheating. Yet, I think that college students instinctively knew that what they talked about, they stood a better chance of remembering. That is why they would form discussion groups outside of class. Students should not have to talk outside of class. They should be conversing about the content in class.

Reciprocal teaching and cooperative learning are two of the best ways to have conversations about content. In the original definition of reciprocal teaching (Palincsar & Brown, 1984), the process is as follows: students make predictions about a part of text to be read. Once the text is read, the group's discussion leader has the group discuss questions that have been raised. A group member then summarizes the content read thus far, and others clarify difficult concepts and make predictions about the following portion of text. Then the process continues. However, my definition is much simpler. Stopping during class time and having students reteach what they are learning to a student sitting nearby is time well spent! After all, we learn at least 70% of what we say as we talk about content (Ekwall & Shanker, 1988).

Very little is done in the world of work by oneself. Most jobs are done while working with a team or at the very least, a partner. What better way to help students develop those interpersonal skills that they will

**127**

need in the workplace than by having them complete some tasks in class cooperatively? Remember this motto: *Some of us are better than others of us, but none of us is better than all of us* (Johnson, Johnson, & Holubec, 1994).

## WHY: THEORETICAL FRAMEWORK

In peer-to-peer tutoring, the student doing the teaching is gaining because to teach something is to remember it and the learner is gaining because of the individual instruction that is tailored to them personally (Gregory & Chapman, 2013).

While competition is learned naturally, cooperation has to be taught (Allen & Currie, 2012).

Cooperative learning is one major strategy for creating a culturally responsive classroom for students of poverty and color (Tileston, 2011).

During partner and group work, students learn social skills along with cognitive skills and think at higher levels as they clarify and discuss information (Gregory & Chapman, 2013).

Inhibiting students from talking decreases the likelihood that any new material will be processed and embedded into long-term memory (Hattie, 2009).

Cooperative group activities improve the learning for diverse students because they teach crucial social skills and reinforce concepts by allowing group members to discuss a variety of ideas (Algozzine et al., 2009b).

Because humans are social beings, working collaboratively elicits thinking that is superior to individual effort (Costa, 2008).

"Share what you know and feel memories grow" (Sprenger, 2007a, p.115).

The total effects of peers teaching one another in class is quite powerful since this technique helps with self-regulation and students being in control of their own learning (Hattie, 2009).

When individuals work together they are able to agree or disagree, state various perspectives, point out and settle differences, and examine alternatives (Costa, 2008).

Individual students' abilities can be nurtured when those students, with or without learning disabilities, belong to a community of learners who engage in peer tutoring and working collaboratively to make sense of mathematics (Posamentier & Jaye, 2006).

Without the metacognitive process of group debriefing following a cooperative activity, there is only minimal improvement in the group's ability to use a specific collaborative or social skill (Gregory & Parry, 2006).

Diversity (mixing boys and girls and high and low achievers) within a cooperative group results in a better exchange of ideas (Feinstein, 2004).

People learn . . .

    10% of what they read

    20% of what they hear

    30% of what they see

    50% of what they both see and hear

    70% of what they say as they talk

    90% of what they say as they do a thing (Ekwall & Shanker 1988, p. 370)

# HOW: INSTRUCTIONAL ACTIVITIES

| | |
|---|---|
| **WHO:** | Elementary/Middle/High |
| **WHEN:** | Before, during, or after a lesson |
| **CONTENT AREA(S):** | Cross-curricular |

• When students are working with peers in small groups or talking to a partner, it is often difficult to get their attention. Create a signal and use it whenever you need students to pay attention to you. The signal can be a chime, raised hand, rain stick, chant, bell, clap, or anything soothing that would not be abrasive to the brains of your students. Change the signal periodically since student brains appreciate novelty.

| | |
|---|---|
| **WHO:** | Elementary/Middle/High |
| **WHEN:** | During a lesson |
| **CONTENT AREA(S):** | Cross-curricular |

• There is a technique I use called *My Turn, Your Turn*. Since the brain can only pay conscious attention to one thing at a time, tell students that when you are addressing the class, this is considered the teacher's turn to talk. This time would be called *My Turn*. When the time comes for students to talk to a partner or a cooperative group, this time would be considered *Your Turn*.

| | |
|---|---|
| **WHO:** | Elementary/Middle/High |
| **WHEN:** | Before a lesson |
| **CONTENT AREA(S):** | Cross-curricular |

• I am often asked how teachers keep students on task when they are allowed to talk to a partner or in a cooperative group. The tactic *of My Stuff, Your Stuff* has worked for me. Tell students that when they are given an assignment, that is considered the teacher's stuff. Students should attend to the teacher's stuff first and be prepared in case they are called upon. Then, if time permits, partners or groups can talk about anything they choose. This conversation would be considered *Your Stuff*. When students know that they may have the opportunity to talk about what they wish, they are more likely to concentrate on what the teacher wants first. According to Allen (2008), it is natural for student conversations to get off the topic. Adults in my workshops do so as well! He suggests letting them finish their personal discussion and then having them bring the conversation back around to the topic at hand.

**WHO:**                  Elementary/Middle/High
**WHEN:**               During a lesson
**CONTENT AREA(S):**       Cross-curricular

- Have each student select a close partner (CP), a peer who sits so close in class that he or she can talk with this person, whenever necessary, and not have to get out of his or her seat. Stop periodically during a lesson and have students discuss a concept, brainstorm an idea, or review content prior to a test. Close partners can also re-explain a concept that might not be clear or easily understood by their partner. According to Gregory and Parry (2006), children learn best when they have the opportunity to discuss ideas with their peers in a nose-to-nose and toes-to-toes interaction.

**WHO:**                  Elementary/Middle/High
**WHEN:**               During a lesson
**CONTENT AREA(S):**       Cross-curricular

- Consult Strategy 10 ("Movement") for a way to integrate reciprocal teaching with movement by having students make clock, seasonal, timeline, or quadrant appointments to discuss pertinent content.

**WHO:**                  Elementary/Middle/High
**WHEN:**               During a lesson
**CONTENT AREA(S):**       Cross-curricular

- Have students work together in cooperative groups, or *families*, of four to six students. They may be seated in groups already or taught to pick up their desks and arrange them into groups for a cooperative-learning activity and to put them back once the activity is over. It is recommended that the groups be of mixed ability levels or capitalize on the various multiple intelligences or talents of students.

**WHO:**                  Elementary/Middle/High
**WHEN:**               During a lesson
**CONTENT AREA(S):**       Cross-curricular

- Give each cooperative group of students the same task. Have them discuss the thought processes involved in completing the task and reach consensus as to the correct answer. Once the answer is agreed upon, have each person in the group sign the paper that the answer is written on, verifying that they agree with the answer and, if called on randomly, could explain how the solution was derived to the entire class. This individual accountability helps to ensure that one person does not do all the work while other students watch and applaud their efforts.

**WHO:**                        Elementary/Middle/High
**WHEN:**                       During a lesson
**CONTENT AREA(S):**            Cross-curricular

• When students have difficulty working together as a cooperative group, you may want to teach some social skills necessary for effective functioning. For example, construct a T-chart similar to the one below where each social skill is considered from two perspectives: (1) what it looks like and (2) what it sounds like. Social skills could include the following: paying undivided attention, encouraging one another, or critiquing ideas and not peers.

Observe each group and make a tally mark on a sheet every time the social skill is practiced by any student in the group. Provide feedback to the class during a debriefing following the cooperative activity. You may also assign a student in each group to fulfill the function of a *process observer* who collects the data for the group. The process observer cannot talk and only observes the group. Therefore, it may be beneficial to make your more talkative student in each group the process observer (Tate, 2014a).

## Paying Attention

| Looks Like | Sounds Like |
|---|---|
| Eye contact | One person speaking at a time |
| Leaning forward | Asking appropriate questions |
| One person speaking | Paraphrasing what is being said |
| Not distracted | Summarizing what is being said |

**Figure 13.1**

**WHO:**                        Elementary/Middle/High
**WHEN:**                       During a lesson
**CONTENT AREA(S):**            Cross-curricular

• Another way to help ensure individual accountability is to assign group roles for students to fulfill during the cooperative learning activity. Some of the following roles can be assigned:

  o **Facilitator**—Ensures that the group stays on task and completes the given activity
  o **Scribe**—Writes down anything the group has to submit in writing

  ○ **Time Keeper**—Tells the group when half the time is over and when there is one minute remaining

  ○ **Reporter**—Gives an oral presentation to the class regarding the results of the group's work

  ○ **Materials Manager**—Collects any materials or other resources that the group needs to complete the task

  ○ **Process Observer**—Provides feedback to the group on how well they practiced their social skills during the cooperative learning activity

| | |
|---|---|
| **WHO:** | Elementary/Middle/High |
| **WHEN:** | During a lesson |
| **CONTENT AREA(S):** | Cross-curricular |

- One way to have students navigate through narrative or expository text is to have them engage in *partner reading*. Students could take turns participating in the *3-Ps* by reading a *page, paragraph*, or *passing* their turn until the selection is complete. They could take turns quizzing their partners regarding what was just read.

| | |
|---|---|
| **WHO:** | Elementary/Middle/High |
| **WHEN:** | During a lesson |
| **CONTENT AREA(S):** | Cross-curricular |

- When students need to memorize facts in any content area, have them pair with a *drill partner*. Students work together to drill one another on the content (such as multiplication facts or content-area vocabulary definitions) for several minutes each day until both partners know and can recite the facts from memory. Give bonus points on the subsequent test if both partners score above a certain percentage or improve their score over a previous test.

| | |
|---|---|
| **WHO:** | Elementary/Middle/High |
| **WHEN:** | During a lesson |
| **CONTENT AREA(S):** | Cross-curricular |

- Have students use the *think, pair, share* technique. Students first individually *think* how they would respond to a question or solve a problem; then they *pair* with another student and *share* their thought processes and/or answer to the problem. Both students reach consensus as to the correct solution or answer. If their original answers differ, the discussion involved in convincing their partner that they are correct is invaluable to learning.

| | |
|---|---|
| **WHO:** | Elementary/Middle/High |
| **WHEN:** | During a lesson |
| **CONTENT AREA(S):** | Cross-curricular |

- Place students in cooperative groups. Have them participate in an activity called *jigsaw*. *Jigsaw's* name is derived from the fact that each student has only one piece of the puzzle, and it will take all students to make a whole. Each student in the cooperative group is accountable for teaching one section of a chapter. The procedure is as follows:

o   Give students time to prepare their part individually either in class or for homework.

o   Have them confer with a student in another group, who has the same part they do, to get and give ideas prior to teaching their original group.

o   Give each student a required number of minutes to teach their part to their original cooperative group. Individuals in each group start and stop teaching at the same time. If they finish before time is called, the student can quiz group members for understanding.

o   Conduct a whole class review that outlines the pertinent points that should have been made during each student's instruction. In this way, the entire class gets to hear the content at least twice, once from a group member and once from the teacher.

**WHO:**                  Elementary/Middle/High
**WHEN:**                 During a lesson
**CONTENT AREA(S):**      Cross-curricular

• While checking a homework or in-class assignment or brainstorming ideas, have students take their paper in hand and walk around the room to fast-paced music. Every time you stop the music, have each student pair with another student standing close by and *give* one answer to their partner and *get* one answer from their partner. Repeat the procedure for a specified period of time or until the song has ended.

## REFLECTION AND APPLICATION

How will I incorporate *reciprocal teaching and cooperative learning* into instruction to engage students' brains?

Which reciprocal teaching and cooperative learning activities am I already integrating as I teach the curriculum?

What additional activities will I integrate?

# Strategy 14

# Role Plays, Drama, Pantomimes, and Charades

## WHAT: DEFINING THE STRATEGY

I go into classrooms when requested and teach model lessons to the students. Teachers observe the lesson while I use brain-compatible strategies to provide instruction on a concept that the teacher is teaching. During one lesson in an American History class, I was asked to teach some vocabulary words that students will need to comprehend prior to their lesson on labor unions. Certainly I could have lectured the students on the words and their definitions. However, that would not only have been boring but I would have been the one doing the work. After all, the person doing the most work is growing the most brain cells or dendrites! In every instance, that should be the students.

I decided to put the vocabulary words and definitions on cards. I divided the class into groups, or *families*, of four and gave each group one vocabulary word. Students were given an assignment to create a role play defining the word in a way that students would never forget it! The words included *strike, Marxism, lockout, boycott*, and so on. My favorite role play involved the word *lockout*. One person in the family locked the remaining members outside of the classroom door and refused to let them back in the room until the demands of the company were met. The family members beat on the door making statements like, "I need this job. I have a family to feed!" or "You can't do this! It is so unfair!" I am pretty sure that when the time comes for the test, most, if not all, students will recall the definition because of the time-tested strategy of role play!

## WHY: THEORETICAL FRAMEWORK

When students are engaged in drama, specific areas of the cerebrum focus on acquiring spoken language while calling on the emotional control center of the brain known as the limbic system (Sousa & Pilecki, 2013).

Role play is a form of rehearsal that enables students to demonstrate skills and process their knowledge in an emotional context (Gregory & Chapman, 2013).

Drama, such as theatrics, storytelling, and having students act out, would be one of nine creative strategies to help students remember new information (Allen & Scozzi, 2012).

The roles that students take on immerse them in situations as they assume the persona of the character they are portraying (Gregory & Chapman, 2013).

The brain-based learning strategies of role play and simulations provide students with emotional connections to real life (Karten, 2008).

In simulation or role-play contexts, learning is more enjoyable and meaningful, choice and creativity come into play, and pressure from negative evaluation is minimized (Jensen, 2008).

Test scores for classes where students were involved in mini-dramas or vignettes were significantly higher than scores in three additional classes taught next door with traditional methods (Allen, 2008).

Role play can be used to reinforce learning in a mathematics class. Examples would include having students make change or take measurements (Sprenger, 2007a).

Role plays are most effective when illustrating key events, demonstrating critical roles of historical figures, and showing the process of concepts that come in sequential order (Udvari-Solner & Kluth, 2008).

Role play motivates students to participate, enhances enthusiasm and recall of information, and stores that information in the body as well as the brain (Jensen, 2007).

As students involve their bodies in the comprehension of concepts and ideas through role plays and skits, they are able to understand the material in a new way (Sprenger, 2007a).

Role plays use visual, spatial, linguistic, and bodily modalities, and, therefore, not only access students' emotions but also enable students to comprehend at much deeper levels than a lecture would (Gregory & Parry, 2006).

## HOW: INSTRUCTIONAL ACTIVITIES

**WHO:**                          Elementary/Middle/High
**WHEN:**                         During a lesson
**CONTENT AREA(S):**              Cross-curricular

- Follow the steps below when engaging students in a simulation or role play:
    - Define what a role play or simulation is and present the topic that is to be role played.
    - Give students the procedures, rules, roles, scoring, and goals of the role play.
    - Monitor, facilitate, and provide feedback as students work through the role play.
    - Debrief the activity and have students discuss how to apply what they learned during the role play (Gregory & Herndon, 2010).

| | |
|---|---|
| **WHO:** | Elementary/Middle/High |
| **WHEN:** | During a lesson |
| **CONTENT AREA(S):** | Cross-curricular |

- Have students *body spell* the letters of their content-area vocabulary words. First, have them visualize the word. Then have them move their bodies according to the placement of the letters in the word. For example, let's suppose the word we need to spell is *play*. The lowercase *p* in *play* falls below the line so to body spell it, the student should bend toward the floor from the waist with the arms extended as if to touch the toes. The *l* in *play* extends above the line so to body spell it, students should put both arms up and reach for the sky. The *a* in *play* falls on the line, so the student should put both arms out to the side. Finally, the *y* in *play* falls below the line (just like the *p*) so the arms are once again positioned to touch the toes. The student then puts it all together and spells the entire word, *play*. They say each letter of the word as they body spell it. Once students learn the technique, they can spell any word. Have them spell content-area vocabulary such as *Mississippi* or *photosynthesis*. As students become more confident with their body spelling, they enjoy spelling words faster and faster, and because the words are being placed in procedural memory, their spelling during writing improves.

| | |
|---|---|
| **WHO:** | Elementary/Middle/High |
| **WHEN:** | During a lesson |
| **CONTENT AREA:** | Mathematics/Social studies |

- Have students develop and participate in a simulated economic system for the classroom where they are asked to design their own classroom currency and create a system for using the currency to buy and sell goods and services for the classroom (Tate, 2012).

| | |
|---|---|
| **WHO:** | Elementary/Middle/High |
| **WHEN:** | During a lesson |
| **CONTENT AREA:** | Mathematics |

- To more clearly understand the steps in a multistep word problem, have students take turns getting up and acting out each step of the word problem. This role play will work with a large majority of math problems and can go a long way in helping students who need a visual depiction of the problem.

| | |
|---|---|
| **WHO:** | Elementary/Middle/High |
| **WHEN:** | During a lesson |
| **CONTENT AREA:** | Social studies |

• Following a lesson on a major historical event, such as the signing of the Declaration of Independence or the Gettysburg Address, have students create and present a dramatic presentation of the event, incorporating major characters and details in sequential order.

| | |
|---|---|
| **WHO:** | Elementary |
| **WHEN:** | During a lesson |
| **CONTENT AREA(S):** | Science |

• Have students show their understanding of a biological process, such as digestion, or a process of nature, such as the rotation and revolution of the planets, by acting it out. For example, divide students into groups of nine. One student in each group pretends to be the sun and stands in the middle of a circle. The other eight form a circle and revolve around the sun in order from closest to the sun to farthest from the sun while simultaneously rotating on their axis. Give students signs to hold up for the planets that they represent so that other students have a visual.

| | |
|---|---|
| **WHO:** | Elementary/Middle/High |
| **WHEN:** | During a lesson |
| **CONTENT AREA(S):** | Language arts |

• Have students participate in *Reader's Theater* by dramatizing a story previously read. Assign parts to members of the class and have them act out their respective parts. This role play goes a long way toward improving comprehension of narrative text. I had a group of eighth-graders do a role play of one scene from *The Outsiders*. They did a wonderful job and made the text so much more memorable!

| | |
|---|---|
| **WHO:** | Elementary/Middle/High |
| **WHEN:** | During a lesson |
| **CONTENT AREA(S):** | Mathematics |

• Teach geometric terms ensuring that students understand their meanings—terms such as *line, line segment, ray, right angle, obtuse angle,* and *acute angle.* Show students an action for each definition. Then have students stand up beside their desks and role play the definitions that you just demonstrated. For example, to demonstrate the term *line,* have students point both arms out to their sides and point their fingers to indicate that a line has no end points. To demonstrate *line segment,* have them point their arms straight out but ball their fingers into fists to demonstrate that a line segment has two end points. Have them demonstrate a *ray* by pointing the arms out and making the left fingers into a fist while pointing the right fingers out straight because the ray only has one end point. Students can role play angles by extending both arms to simulate right, obtuse, and acute angles. Involve students in a game by having them use their arms to make the terms as you randomly say them. This game is a lot of fun while putting the terms into procedural or muscle memory.

**WHO:**  Middle/High
**WHEN:**  During a lesson
**CONTENT AREA(S):**  English/Social studies

   • Following a discussion of the judicial system, have students establish a peer court in which they try a character in a novel or a historical figure for a predetermined offense. Roles of the judge, bailiff, jury, witnesses, prosecuting attorney, and defense attorney are assigned and carried out by members of the class.

**WHO:**  Elementary/Middle/High
**WHEN:**  During a lesson
**CONTENT AREA(S):**  Cross-curricular

   • Have students take turns role playing that they are you, the teacher. Have them volunteer to come to the front of the room and pretend, as the teacher, to reteach the lesson previously taught. Give each student a maximum of two minutes. This activity will give you an idea of which concepts have been understood by your students and which may need reteaching. Remember that you learn what you teach and that most brains need to hear something a minimum of three times before the information actually sticks. As a side benefit, you will get to see your teaching through your students' eyes. At the end of one lesson I taught, I had a fourth-grader come to the front of the room and reteach what I had taught about solving multistep math word problems. I went and sat in the student's desk. When it was time for me to get up, I couldn't! I was literally stuck in the fourth-grade desk. We had a good laugh about that one!

## REFLECTION AND APPLICATION

> **How will I incorporate *role plays, drama, pantomimes, and charades* into instruction to engage students' brains?**

**Which role plays, drama, pantomimes, and charades am I already integrating as I teach the curriculum?**

**What additional activities will I integrate?**

# Strategy 15

## Storytelling

### WHAT: DEFINING THE STRATEGY

Tell your students the following story to teach the continents. It will take you less than one minute.

---

There once was a man named **North**. His last name was **America**.

He fell in love with a beautiful woman named **South**. They got married and she took his name so she became **South America**. They honeymooned in **Europe**. This couple was blessed to have four daughters whose names all began with the letter *A*. Their names were **Africa**, **Antarctica**, **Asia**, and **Australia**.

The End

---

By the time you have told this story aloud at least three times and students have gotten up and re-told the story to several partners in the room, students remember the continents. Why? Because the continents are not learned in isolation. They are learned within the context of a story. Storytelling, one of the oldest forms of instruction, used to be the only way that people had of passing information from one generation to the next.

If you don't think stories are important to all brains, watch when a speaker or minister tells a story. Everyone gets quiet! However, I don't believe in telling stories that waste instructional time. Every time you tell a story, be sure that it teaches or reviews a concept. When students remember the story, they remember the concept you were trying to teach.

## WHY: THEORETICAL FRAMEWORK

Telling good stories is like weight lifting for the brain since stories force listeners to make connections between their world, feelings, and ideas (Stibich, 2014).

The structure and sequencing of stories make them engaging and a natural way for the brain to think about and process information (Allen & Scozzi, 2012).

People love good stories, whether real or make believe, because stories usually resemble the reality with which we are familiar but find difficult to define (Scott & Marzano, 2014).

Storytelling conveys the plot structure and language of the story that enhances a student's reading comprehension (Marsh, 2013).

When a listener hears a story, the story activates parts of the listener's brain so that the experiences and ideas in the story become those of the listener (Widrich, 2012).

Since stories show how ideas interact, they can be extremely useful as a foundation for helping students think critically (Allen & Scozzi, 2012).

Storytelling is an effective way to enhance a student's emotional connection to the content and conceptual understanding and helps students' *digital brains* become more attentive (Sprenger, 2010).

Students often remember stories better when they create original ones (Allen, 2008).

Children naturally develop a sense of story, and the brain's fascination with story continues throughout our lives (Caine et al., 2005).

Children's favorite stories involve the challenges faced by protagonists who overcome adversity to achieve their goals (Willis, 2007a).

Stories created by teachers can assist students in understanding number operations in a variety of contexts (National Council of Teachers of Mathematics, 2000).

After a period of intense learning, storytelling enables the brain to relax and facilitates the retention of newly acquired material (Jensen, 2000).

## HOW: INSTRUCTIONAL ACTIVITIES

**WHO:**                    Elementary/Middle/High
**WHEN:**                   Before or during a lesson
**CONTENT AREA(S):**        Cross-curricular

• Have a story stool or bench in your classroom and sit on it every time you tell students stories related to a concept being taught. No notes are taken during storytelling so that students can give their undivided attention to you in this nonthreatening environment. Remember, never tell a story unless its purpose is to teach or reinforce a curricular concept to be remembered. Warren Phillips, exemplary science teacher, used his story bench regularly and held students rapt attention with his stories about science concepts.

| | |
|---|---|
| **WHO:** | Elementary/Middle/High |
| **WHEN:** | During a lesson |
| **CONTENT AREA(S):** | Cross-curricular |

• The brain needs a purpose. Whenever giving students either narrative or informational text to read silently or orally, always give them the purpose for reading. For example, say to students, *We are reading the next two pages to find out why . . .*

| | |
|---|---|
| **WHO:** | Elementary/Middle/High |
| **WHEN:** | During a lesson |
| **CONTENT AREA(S):** | Cross-curricular |

• Create stories, factual or fictional, that can be used to illustrate a cross-curricular concept that you are teaching. Integrate the stories into your lesson delivery and watch students more easily retain the concept. If your story is humorous or emotional, the recall value is enhanced. For example, use the following cross-curricular stories to teach students to remember the 13 original colonies in social studies (written by Gloria Caracas, El Oro Way Elementary School) and the concept of natural selection in science (written by Warren Phillips, Plymouth Middle School).

  o There once was a cow named <u>Georgette</u> **(Georgia)**. She was a <u>Jersey</u> **(New Jersey)** cow and gave lots of milk. She was strange because she liked to wear yellow <u>underwear</u> **(Delaware)**. One day, she went up the <u>Empire State Building</u> **(New York)**. Up there she sang two Christmas <u>carols</u> **(North Carolina, South Carolina)**. Then she came down and walked down the <u>road</u> **(Rhode Island)**. She was carrying a <u>massive</u> **(Massachusetts)** <u>Virginia</u> **(Virginia)** <u>ham</u> **(New Hampshire)**. She bent down to pick up a <u>pencil</u> **(Pennsylvania)** and proceeded to do a <u>connect-a-dot</u> **(Connecticut)** of <u>Marilyn</u> **(Maryland)** Monroe (Tate, 2012, pp. 121–122).
  o The light-colored form of the moth was the predominant form in England prior to the beginning of the industrial revolution. Then darker-colored forms of the moth became much more prevalent. In areas where pollution had darkened the landscape, the darker moths were better camouflaged and less likely to be eaten by birds. Later, after the use of coal declined, under less-polluted conditions, the light-colored moths prevailed again. Go figure! (Tate & Phillips, 2011, p. 125).

| WHO: | Elementary/Middle/High |
| WHEN: | During a lesson |
| CONTENT AREA(S): | Cross-curricular |

- Have students create stories, fictional or factual, that can be used to remember a concept that has been taught. Stories are particularly helpful when recalling a multistep process or events that happen in sequential order. Have students retell their stories several times to their classmates. Have them recall their original stories each time they attempt to remember the key concept on which the story is based.

| WHO: | Elementary/Middle |
| WHEN: | During a lesson |
| CONTENT AREA(S): | Mathematics |

- Read aloud to the class any of the appropriate books in the bibliography, *Have You Read Any Math Lately?* found on page 147 of *Mathematics Worksheets Don't Grow Dendrites: 20 Numeracy Strategies That Engage the Brain* (Tate, 2009). These include Neuschwander's series of books about *Sir Cumference* and Scieszka's book, *Math Curse*. The first time you read the books aloud, do so for the enjoyment of the literature. Then revisit the book at another time and select a math skill or strategy from the story. The context of the story will help students remember the skill being taught.

| WHO: | Elementary/Middle/High |
| WHEN: | During a lesson |
| CONTENT AREA(S): | Language arts |

- Select literary works that contain numerous examples of language arts skills and strategies from the curriculum to be taught. Although a few titles are listed below as examples, any story or poem that contains examples of the skill can be used. Read the story or poem aloud to the class initially for enjoyment. Reread parts of the story on a subsequent day, pointing out examples of the skill or strategy to be taught. Have students look for examples in this or other literary works.

| Title | Author | Concepts |
| --- | --- | --- |
| *The Important Book* | Margaret Wise Brown | Main idea and details |
| *The Day Jimmy's Boa Ate the Wash* | Trinka Hayes Noble | Cause and effect |
| *Thomas' Snowsuit* | Robert Munsch | Sequence of events |
| *The Pain and the Great One* | Judy Blume | Point of view |
| *Encounter* | Jane Yolen | Point of view |
| *My Brother's Flying Machine* | Jane Yolen | Point of view |
| *The King Who Rained* | Fred Gwynne | Figurative language |
| *Amelia Bedelia* series | Judy Blume | Figurative language |

| Title | Author | Concepts |
|---|---|---|
| *The Parts of Speech* series | Brian Cleary | Parts of speech |
| *The Parts of Speech* series | Ruth Heller | Parts of speech |
| *The Doorbell Rang* | Pat Hutchins | Concept of division |
| *Counting on Frank* | Rod Clement | Real-world math |
| *Math Curse* | John Scieszka | Real-world math |
| *Science Alphabet Books* series | Jerry Pallotta | Science concepts |

**WHO:**            Elementary/Middle/High
**WHEN:**           During a lesson
**CONTENT AREA(S):**  Cross-curricular

- Following a read-aloud or the silent reading of a story or content-area unit of study, have students retell the story to a partner with story events in the correct sequential order.

**WHO:**            Elementary/Middle/High
**WHEN:**           During a lesson
**CONTENT AREA(S):**  Cross-curricular

- Have students work individually or in cooperative groups to use the *narrative chaining* method by creating an original story linking together unrelated terms, concepts, or words in a list.

**WHO:**            Elementary/Middle/High
**WHEN:**           Before or during a lesson
**CONTENT AREA(S):**  Mathematics

- Consult the text *Math and Children's Literature*, which provides numerous examples of stories that can be used to teach various math principles. Refer to the index of the *Math and Children's Literature* book to find children's books that will teach or reinforce a concept being taught.

**WHO:**            Middle/High
**WHEN:**           During a lesson
**CONTENT AREA(S):**  Mathematics

- Tell students "The Story of the Algebraic Equation" to help them understand one step in solving equations. This story also incorporates the strategies of movement, role play, and metaphor. Seven students hold cards that represent the numbers and signs in the algebraic equation $3y + 10 = 2y + 18$. $3y$ and $2y$ should be female students. *Ten* and *18* should be male students. The cards for *10* and *2y* should have $-10$ and $-2y$ written on the backs, respectively. Students role play the story as it is read.

# "The Story of the Algebraic Equation"

$$3y + 10 = 2y + 18$$

Once upon a time, there were two families that lived on either side of a busy street called Equal Street. Each family had two children (one teenage daughter and one younger son). One day the teenage daughters, 3y and 2y, made a date to go to the mall. However, there was a problem. Each daughter had been asked to babysit a younger brother. 3y had to babysit 10 and 2y had to babysit 18.

The girls desperately wanted to get together to go to the mall. Therefore, daughter 3y suggested that she send her younger brother 10 to cross Equal Street so that he could play with her friend's brother, 18. Now, there was one peculiar thing about this particular town. Whenever anyone crossed Equal Street, they had to turn around and cross it backward. So younger brother 10 turned backward and crossed the street. The two boys were very happy because now they could play together.

There was only one problem. To be all alone with no one to bother them, the boys had to get rid of big sister 2y. That was all right with big sister 2y because she wanted to go to the mall with her friend 3y anyway. So she said good-bye to her brother and crossed Equal Street, backward of course, and she and her friend 3y could be all alone to proceed to the mall. The girls had a wonderful time and so did the boys.

When the girls returned from the mall, they were in a world of trouble because their parents had told them over and over again never to leave their younger brothers unattended. But you know as well as I do that for generations older sisters have left younger brothers unattended. That's just the way the story goes!

———————————

## REFLECTION AND APPLICATION

> ### How will I incorporate *storytelling* into instruction to engage students' brains?

**Which storytelling activities am I already integrating as I teach the curriculum?**

**What additional activities will I integrate?**

# Strategy 16

# Technology

## WHAT: DEFINING THE STRATEGY

One of my favorite commercials is one for Walmart where a father surprises his teenage daughter with her own cell phone. In her euphoric state, she excitedly hugs her father and announces to him that she will now be able to "pin, post, tweet, snap, tag, check, and share." In a nutshell, she provided a summary of the many things that students today can readily do via technology.

Students are what Prensky (2009) calls "digital natives." Most have never known life without technology. Eighty-nine percent of 18- to 24-year-old

"This isn't a good time. I'm in trouble with the Dean for using a cell phone in class. I'll call you back."

SOURCE: Bacall (2003a).

153

Americans are online. Students ages 12 to 24 will spend more than four hours a day viewing media, not including games. Eighty-two percent of seventh- to twelfth-graders even "media multitask" while simultaneously doing homework (Frontline, 2010, n.p.). I, on the other hand, am a "digital immigrant" (Prensky, 2009) and though I was late to learn to google, my children now call me the *google queen*. I search Google for everything—the weather in a city to which I will be going, the score of a sporting event, or a topic that I must teach when planning a model lesson.

Technological advances have revolutionized all aspects of our lives, including how educators teach and students learn. Technological literacy is crucial and one of the five competencies that high school students should be proficient with if they are to be successful in the work world (Secretary's Commission on Achieving Necessary Skills [SCANS], 1991). This strategy will deal with the amazing and engaging impact that can be made on a lesson when technology is integrated.

However, the longer I am around today's students, the more convinced I am that the strategy of technology should be considered only one of 20, and needs to be balanced with the other 19. A combination of strategies helps to foster the interpersonal skills that are essential for meaningful personal and professional relationships in the real world. Too many students are so caught up in text messaging and e-mailing others that they have lost the art of true interpersonal communication. For example, I saw an announcement in a university catalog for a new course being offered, titled Interpersonal Communication. In small type, underneath the title were the following words: *This class will be taught online.* I don't know about you but, to me, that seems like an oxymoron.

## WHY: THEORETICAL FRAMEWORK

Infusing *digital literacy* within each content area not only teaches relevant subject matter with 21st century technology but also addresses vital literacy skills emphasized in the Common Core (Summey, 2013).

Students become excited and challenged to find answers to problems and create unique ways of presenting information when they are allowed to use their gadgets at appropriate times (Gregory & Chapman, 2013).

"A 21st century classroom looks to engage learners in collaborative groups, where learning takes place in and out of school" (Covili, 2012).

Students of all ability levels can use *technology to process, demonstrate, retain and share information and communication* (Karten, 2009, p. 196).

Curriculum can be adjusted and lessons made to fit the specific needs of students with the help of computer technology (Willis, 2006).

Assistive technology can support the participation of students with disabilities in whole class and small group discussion (Udvari-Solner & Kluth, 2008).

Higher achievement and greater understanding in math is achieved when technology is used for non-routine applications and not for routine calculations (Sousa, 2007).

When the inquiry-based learning model is paired with dynamic geometric software programs, students are able to discover relationships, make hypotheses, and defend assumptions (Posamentier & Jaye, 2006).

Technology is not an end unto itself but should be used to enrich, enhance, and present content in a more efficient manner (Sousa, 2011).

Self-paced, interactive, Internet-based K–12 courses enable students to work full- or part-time while simultaneously pursuing their education (Barr & Parrett, 2007).

The use of computers can add a diversity of teaching strategies, increased opportunities for practice, and increases in the nature and amount of feedback to the student (Hattie, 2009).

Interactive technology (such as computer animation or HyperStudio) makes the learning fun and exciting for adolescents (Feinstein, 2004).

Minute online connections with peers through e-mail, Facebook, or Twitter are no substitute for live, face-to-face communication (Sousa & Pilecki, 2013).

Recent results from studies in China found that addiction to the Internet can lower the density of gray matter in the adolescent brain (Park et al., 2011; Zhou et al., 2011).

# HOW: INSTRUCTIONAL ACTIVITIES

**WHO:**             Elementary/Middle/High
**WHEN:**            During a lesson
**CONTENT AREA(S):** Cross-curricular

• Involve students in content with the use of a SMART or Promethean board. These technological presentation devices enable the teacher to access the Internet and display it to the entire class as well as show the class other computer programs of interest. The SMART board can also be used to display regular writing when done with the special markers provided.

**WHO:**             Elementary/Middle/High
**WHEN:**            During a lesson
**CONTENT AREA(S):** Cross-curricular

• Use a piece of technology called a document camera (often referred to as an ELMO) to provide visuals for students. The camera must be connected to an LCD projector and serves a similar function to the old opaque projector, which is now extinct. Anything placed underneath the camera will provide a visual for the class. Therefore, you can use the camera to write notes, work math problems, or show student work to the class. Even if you read a story to the class from a picture book, the pictures will show to the entire class. The document camera can also be connected to a computer for easy toggle back and forth for showing videos or Internet connections. I use a document camera when I present to adult audiences. I love the flexibility it provides that computer programs may not.

**WHO:**                   Elementary/Middle/High
**WHEN:**                  During a lesson
**CONTENT AREA(S):**       Cross-curricular

• I am often asked how to deal with the digital distractions that students' technological devices provide during instruction. My answer is to incorporate those devices into instruction. Plan opportunities for students to use their personal gadgets such as smartphones, e-readers, cameras, tablets, or laptops to accomplish a curricular objective. During those times when these gadgets are not being used, make it a rule to have students put them away so that their conscious attention is not divided.

**WHO:**                   Elementary/Middle/High
**WHEN:**                  During a lesson
**CONTENT AREA(S):**       Cross-curricular

• The following types of technology address the major memory pathways of learners:

  o **Semantic**—mind maps, blogging, texting, searching online
  o **Episodic**—story searches, use of a computer lab setting
  o **Procedural**—step-by-step software programs, PowerPoint presentations, programs with drag-and-drop features, organizational classroom routines
  o **Automatic**—memory games, computerized flashcards, using software to create poems
  o **Emotional**—blogging, texting, group computer time (Sprenger, 2010).

By using a variety of technology types, the memory pathways of all students can be addressed at some points and broadened at other times.

**WHO:**                   Elementary/Middle/High
**WHEN:**                  During or after a lesson
**CONTENT AREA(S):**       Cross-curricular

• Have students access websites, such as Newsela, which allow them to explore news stories at a variety of reading levels and take differentiated quizzes on the stories. Fisher (2013) refers to this instructional strategy as *digital differentiation.* The website Wordle enables teachers to create tag clouds of different news stories. This allows students to compare and contrast the treatment of the same news stories by different news agencies. A service called Newspapermap will compare news stories from the United States with those from around the world (Fisher, 2013).

| | |
|---|---|
| **WHO:** | Elementary/Middle/High |
| **WHEN:** | During or after a lesson |
| **CONTENT AREA(S):** | Cross-curricular |

• Have students use the process of digital storytelling in integrating technology. Have them take photographs or create illustrations that represent either the main idea and details of informational text or the elements of a narrative story. Import these photographs or illustrations into a digital storytelling tool such as iMovie, Movie Maker, or Photo Story. Add narration. Use this activity to motivate struggling writers or ESL students (McLaughlin & Overturf, 2013).

| | |
|---|---|
| **WHO:** | Elementary/Middle/High |
| **WHEN:** | During or after a lesson |
| **CONTENT AREA(S):** | Cross-curricular |

• Have students use multiple digital media and visual displays such as PowerPoint to make oral presentations to the class more interesting and the audience more attentive. These media could include video clips, graphics, sound, and interactive components (Tate, 2014a).

| | |
|---|---|
| **WHO:** | Elementary/Middle/High |
| **WHEN:** | During or after a lesson |
| **CONTENT AREA(S):** | Cross-curricular |

• Allow students to make interactive posters by using Glogster or Thinglink. Students could locate drawings related to the topic they are addressing and add features such as videos, text, voice overs, and additional images to make their posters interactive (Fisher, 2013).

| | |
|---|---|
| **WHO:** | Elementary/Middle/High |
| **WHEN:** | During or after a lesson |
| **CONTENT AREA(S):** | Cross-curricular |

• Even note taking can be digitized. Have individual students use writing apps or software on their computers to save digital versions of their notes, which can be modified and shared by way of e-mail. Apps and tools such as Google Docs, Draftin, and TodaysMeet allow students to contribute notes, media, and hyperlinks to other students in real time (Fisher, 2013).

| | |
|---|---|
| **WHO:** | Elementary/Middle/High |
| **WHEN:** | During a lesson |
| **CONTENT AREA(S):** | Cross-curricular |

- Have students design a Facebook page for a fictional or historical character. The Facebook page should include personal biographical information, a listing of family members, personal likes and dislikes, social affiliations, as well as a timeline of important life events. Students can then decide what other people living at that time would have been Facebook friends with the original character (Tate, 2014a).

**WHO:**                Elementary/Middle/High
**WHEN:**               During a lesson
**CONTENT AREA(S):**    Cross-curricular

- Allow students to complete content-specific projects online. They can use e-portfolios to digitally display their work, receive comments and feedback from the teacher and peers, assess their own progress, and complete their goals (Gregory & Chapman, 2013).

**WHO:**                Middle/High
**WHEN:**               After a lesson
**CONTENT AREA(S):**    Cross-curricular

- Have students create an original song, rhyme, or a rap, as suggested in Strategy 11 ("Music, Rhythm, Rhyme, and Rap"), to demonstrate their understanding of course content. Select the best creative efforts and have those students follow the necessary directions to post their songs, rhymes, or raps on iTunes or YouTube for others to enjoy.

**WHO:**                Elementary/Middle/High
**WHEN:**               During a lesson
**CONTENT AREA(S):**    Cross-curricular

- Have students do role plays or reenactments of content. An online tool, such as Wideo, allows students to take those role plays and make animated movies of them. Students develop their literacy skills as they write the dialogue and are able to interact with characters, settings, elements, and so forth (Fisher, 2013).

## REFLECTION AND APPLICATION

> ### How will I incorporate *technology* into instruction to engage students' brains?

**Which technology activities am I already integrating as I teach the curriculum?**

**What additional activities will I integrate?**

# Strategy 17

# Visualization and Guided Imagery

## WHAT: DEFINING THE STRATEGY

This all-important strategy is used in at least two places in the real world—sports and medicine. Coaches advise players to picture themselves hitting the home run or scoring the touchdown before the game even begins. This practice increases the likelihood that the same action

"My teacher says I'm an underachiever, but I think she's an overexpecter."

SOURCE: Bacall (2003a).

will happen in the game. Doctors often advise their cancer patients who are taking chemotherapy to visualize the chemotherapy medicine knocking out the cancer cells in the body. This strategy seems to increase the effectiveness of the medicine.

Visualization also works for your students and for you. Visualize when you were young and you went outside and played. Remember that you saw yourself as someone else and your friend as another person. The tree in your yard was not a tree, but your house. In other words, you imagined. One reason that some of today's students have a difficult time comprehending what they read is because in this world of vivid visuals found on computer screens and in video games, students have had little opportunity to use their imaginations. And yet if there are no pictures in a novel, good readers have to visualize the action in the story. Otherwise, there is little or no comprehension. This strategy provides opportunities for students to use their imaginations to facilitate understanding across the curriculum.

Visualize every one of your students experiencing success this year. This is the first step toward ensuring that it happens!

## WHY: THEORETICAL FRAMEWORK

When the brain imagines, it releases endorphins that increase the size of the brain by growing new dendrites and speeds communication within and between brain cells (Marsh, 2013).

Building visual imagery into a story being told increases the retention rate of the story (Allen & Scozzi, 2012).

If a student visualizes what is heard, their ability to visualize what they read is increased (Marsh, 2013).

Since visualized note taking combines on-paper verbal information in sequence with symbols and visual patterns, it is a strategy that associates language with visual imagery (Sousa, 2011).

When important events in history are too abstract to remember, visual imagery facilitates the retention of those events (Melber & Hunter, 2010).

"If a picture is worth a thousand words, perhaps drawing and visualization can help science students enhance their learning potential" (National Science Teachers Association [NSTA], 2006, p. 20).

Like great athletes (e.g., skiers and golfers) and actors, students can visualize a performance before it happens (Caine et al., 2005).

Visualization enhances learning and retention of information because, during mental imagery, the same sections of the brain's visual cortex are activated than when the eyes are actually processing input from the real world (Sousa, 2006).

In a study at Oxford University, one group of elementary students was asked to visualize prior to testing, whereas a second group simply took the test. The group that visualized prior to testing scored higher (Drake, 1996).

The image is the greatest instrument of instruction. If the majority of classroom time was spent ensuring that students are forming proper images, the instructor's work would be indefinitely facilitated (Dewey, 1938).

# HOW: INSTRUCTIONAL ACTIVITIES

**WHO:**            Elementary/Middle/High
**WHEN:**           Before a lesson
**CONTENT AREA(S):** Cross-curricular

• Students in every classroom should visualize themselves being successful! That visualization helps to build confidence and, since success builds success, teachers need to do everything within their power to help students experience those initial positive experiences. It even worked for me. I visualized every one of my eight books as bestsellers. Seven of eight books are bestsellers! One teacher related to me that at the beginning of every school year, she has students write the word *can't* on a piece of paper and then ball it up and throw it into the trash. Then she teaches them this motto: *Success comes in cans, not in can'ts!* After all, *If you believe you can or you believe you can't, you're right!*

**WHO:**            Elementary/Middle/High
**WHEN:**           During a lesson
**CONTENT AREA(S):** Mathematics

• To provide practice in visualizing, as you read a word problem aloud, have students imagine each step of the problem. Have them see in their mind what is happening and then determine what operations are needed to solve the problem. Stop periodically and have students draw what they are visualizing. Visualization is one of the strategies students in Singapore are encouraged to use when solving problems. Their test scores speak for themselves!

**WHO:**            Elementary/Middle/High
**WHEN:**           During a lesson
**CONTENT AREA(S):** Cross-curricular

• Read aloud to students at all grade levels for purposes of information, enjoyment, or to teach a skill or strategy. As you read, have students visualize what is happening. Stop periodically and have students describe the scenes in their minds to one another, and then compare them to the original text.

| **WHO:** | Elementary/Middle/High |
| --- | --- |
| **WHEN:** | During a lesson |
| **CONTENT AREA(S):** | Cross-curricular |

• As students read a novel or content-area passage independently, teach them how to visualize the scenes or events using each of their senses. Have them answer the following question: *What do you see, hear, feel, touch, and taste as you visualize the passage you are reading?*

| **WHO:** | Elementary/Middle/High |
| --- | --- |
| **WHEN:** | During a lesson |
| **CONTENT AREA(S):** | Cross-curricular |

• Have students work individually or in groups to create visual images that link a word to its definition or as in social studies, a state to its capital. The more absurd the visual image, the easier it is for the brain to remember the connection. For example, to remember that the capital of Minnesota is St. Paul, have students visualize a saint sipping on a little bitty soda (Tate, 2012).

| **WHO:** | Elementary/Middle/High |
| --- | --- |
| **WHEN:** | During a lesson |
| **CONTENT AREA(S):** | Mathematics |

• Have students visualize what a given shape would look like rotated 180 degrees, flipped vertically, or turned 90 degrees. Have them describe or draw the resulting figure.

| **WHO:** | Elementary/Middle/High |
| --- | --- |
| **WHEN:** | During a lesson |
| **CONTENT AREA(S):** | Cross-curricular |

• When students must recall concepts, events, or objects in sequential order in any content area, have them visualize the items in the sequence connected together in novel ways. Have them imagine the items upside down, backwards, being tossed about, crashing into one another, dancing together, or positioned in unique ways. Since these items are being visualized in novel ways, the brain stands a better chance of remembering them. Brains pay attention to novelty (Tate, 2012)!

| **WHO:** | Elementary/Middle/High |
| --- | --- |
| **WHEN:** | During a lesson |
| **CONTENT AREA(S):** | Science |

• As you use guided imagery to orally describe a bodily function, have students visualize themselves involved in the process, such as a red blood cell coursing through the body or a piece of food involved in the process of digestion. As a red blood cell, have them imagine the salty taste, the warm temperature, or the wetness that they would experience.

**WHO:**                     Elementary/Middle/High
**WHEN:**                    During a lesson
**CONTENT AREA(S):**         Physical education

- To improve the quality of their physical performance, have students visualize themselves being successful, such as getting the base hit, making the basket, completing the pass, or jumping the farthest. These positive images help to increase confidence in the brain and improve physical prowess. When the confidence level in sports changes from one team to another, that is known as a momentum shift and often results in a positive change in the score of the game for the team that is now the most confident.

**WHO:**                     Elementary/Middle/High
**WHEN:**                    During a lesson
**CONTENT AREA(S):**         Social studies

- Have students mentally transport themselves into a specific period of history being studied, such as the Civil War or the French Revolution, and visualize themselves in that period. Have them ask and answer the following questions: What do you see? How are you dressed? What's going on around you? These images will help to make history more relevant and memorable.

**WHO:**                     Elementary/Middle/High
**WHEN:**                    During a lesson
**CONTENT AREA(S):**         Cross-curricular

- Show students a content-area visual such as a math formula, vocabulary word, or science process. After a period of time, remove the visual and ask them to visualize the concept and write it from memory. Repeat the process several times since the brain needs that repetition.

**WHO:**                     Elementary/Middle/High
**WHEN:**                    During a lesson
**CONTENT AREA(S):**         Cross-curricular

- To alleviate anxiety prior to any test, have students take deep breaths and visualize themselves successfully completing each item on the test. This activity, in addition to well-taught lessons incorporating the brain-compatible strategies, gives students the confidence they need to do well!

## REFLECTION AND APPLICATION

How will I incorporate *visualization and guided imagery*
into instruction to engage students' brains?

Which visualization and guided imagery activities am I already
integrating as I teach the curriculum?

What additional activities will I integrate?

# Strategy 18

# Visuals

## WHAT: DEFINING THE STRATEGY

Have you flown in an airplane recently? If so, you will remember that it is not sufficient for the flight attendants to simply *tell* you what to do with your seat belt and the other myriad instructions they need to give. They have to show you. They either get out in the aisle and demonstrate while holding the apparatus or show you what to do via a video. Why? Even airline personnel know that merely telling human beings what they need to know is probably the least effective form of getting the information across to them. Brains need a visual to accompany the information. I fly so frequently that not only have I memorized the dialogue of what to do but also I can actually physically show you where the exits are. If you ever attend one of my workshops, I will be more than happy to demonstrate this crucial information for you (smile). Airlines, like Southwest and Delta, have even added the strategy of *humor* to the flight instructions to increase the passengers' attention and retention.

The Chinese knew the power of visuals thousands of years ago when they created the following proverb:

*Tell me, I forget.*

*Show me, I remember.*

*Involve me, I understand!*

At least 50% of students in any classroom will be predominately visual learners (Willis, 2006). Look at all of the information that today's students are taking in visually. They are texting on their cell phones, they are playing video games; they are spending hours on the Internet; or they are watching television. These activities would make the visual modality a strong one for many of your students. There is even physical evidence to support

**169**

that the visual cortex in the brains of students today is actually physically thicker than it was in my brain when I was their age. That is why you need the strategy of visuals.

## WHY: THEORETICAL FRAMEWORK

Reality or fantasy can be created with the same ease by the internal visual processing system of the brain (Sousa & Pilecki, 2013).

"The brain processes visuals up to 60,000 times faster than words" (Gregory & Chapman, 2013, p. 23).

When constructing visuals, text should be kept to a minimum and too many visuals per slide avoided (Allen & Scozzi, 2012).

Thinking with visuals (murals, drawings, computer graphics, and paintings) is an effective tool for elaboration because words along with pictures can show great detail (Jensen, 2009b).

Visual aids provide students with a point of focus and improve learning as students encounter the following stages of acquiring new concepts: acquisition, proficiency, maintenance, and generalization (Algozzine et al., 2009b).

Visuals can often help to communicate a teacher's message in a more powerful way than words because visuals can be taken in quickly and remembered by the brain (Allen, 2008).

Because the eyes can take in 30 million bits of information per second, teachers should provide images and moving pictures when instructing students (Jensen, 2007).

Concept maps, flowcharts, graphic icons, cartoons, sketches, and drawings are all visuals that help students understand and process new content (Allen, 2008).

Visual learners take in the world through pictures and words and need to see the teacher solve a problem first to understand it (Sprenger, 2007a).

For English learners, visual tools in math offer visual ways of thinking about relationships and communicating information (Coggins et al., 2007).

After about two weeks, the effects of direct instruction diminish on the brains of students, but the effects of visuals and those images taken in peripherally continue to increase during the same period of time (Jensen, 2007).

When visuals and the auditory information used to explain those visuals go together, they can be helpful. Otherwise, pictures can interfere with a person's ability to listen to the words (Posamentier & Jaye, 2006).

Even though rote learning plays some part, students in Singapore comprehend abstract concepts by using visual tools (Prystay, 2004).

# HOW: INSTRUCTIONAL ACTIVITIES

**WHO:**                          Elementary/Middle/High
**WHEN:**                         During a lesson
**CONTENT AREA(S):**              Cross-curricular

• Gain and keep students' visual attention by changing your location in the room. Begin your lesson in the front of the class and then shift to other areas. This tactic will not only keep students interested but also put you in close proximity to all students and communicate to them that you care about their well-being and are interested in what they are doing. *Remember to teach on your feet, not in your seat!*

**WHO:**                          Elementary/Middle/High
**WHEN:**                         Before a lesson
**CONTENT AREA(S):**              Cross-curricular

• Prior to reading content-area texts, have students survey the chapter or unit of study and peruse any visuals such as maps, charts, graphs, pictures, chapter titles and subtitles, or bold headings. Have them make predictions as to what the chapter or unit will include. This survey technique, called *SQ3R* (Survey, Question, Read, Recite, Review), should facilitate comprehension.

**WHO:**                          Elementary/Middle/High
**WHEN:**                         Before a lesson
**CONTENT AREA(S):**              Cross-curricular

• Place visuals on the classroom bulletin boards and walls that introduce or reinforce concepts being taught. For example, display a visual of the *periodic table* on the wall in a science class or the eight parts of speech in a language arts class. Even if those visuals are removed during testing, they can still be visualized by students.

**WHO:**                          Elementary/Middle/High
**WHEN:**                         During a lesson
**CONTENT AREA(S):**              Cross-curricular

• When lecturing, PowerPoint can be a great visual tool, but it is overused. I have watched students disengage when too many slides are shown. Remember the following 10–20–30 rule of good PowerPoint: (1) no more than 10 slides, (2) no more than 20 minutes, and (3) each line on the slide should be at least 30 font. Remember to intersperse activity within your lecture. Have a miniature copy of your slides for your students since they will not be listening to you if they are simultaneously having to do too much writing.

**WHO:**                          Elementary/Middle/High
**WHEN:**                         During a lesson
**CONTENT AREA(S):**              Cross-curricular

- Facilitate lecture or discussion with visuals by writing key words and phrases or drawing pictures on a dry-erase or SMART board, or on a document camera. For example, write the word "noun" and the words "person," "place," "thing," and "idea" as you explain its definition or draw and label a picture of the heart as you explain its function. Color leaves its imprint on the brain. Write with a blue marker, which works well for most students' brains. Emphasize keys words or phrases in red.

| | |
|---|---|
| **WHO:** | Elementary/Middle/High |
| **WHEN:** | During a lesson |
| **CONTENT AREA(S):** | Cross-curricular |

- As you deliver a lecturette, or minilecture, provide students with a visual by filling in a semantic map or creating an appropriate graphic organizer emphasizing the lecturette's main ideas and key points. Place the map or organizer on the board. Have students draw the visual along with you. Lecturettes typically last less than seven minutes. (See Strategy 5, "Graphic Organizers, Semantic Maps, and Word Webs," for specific examples.)

| | |
|---|---|
| **WHO:** | Elementary/Middle/High |
| **WHEN:** | During a lesson |
| **CONTENT AREA(S):** | Cross-curricular |

- Find and show students a visual or a real artifact to clarify a concept being taught. For example, bring in a live chrysanthemum as you teach the vocabulary word for this flower, show a picture of the Great Wall of China as you teach about its history, or bring in a pizza to teach the concept of fractional pieces.

| | |
|---|---|
| **WHO:** | Elementary/Middle/High |
| **WHEN:** | During a lesson |
| **CONTENT AREA(S):** | Mathematics |

- When introducing a new math concept, work a minimum of three problems on the SMART or dry-erase board or document camera so that all students can see the steps involved. Most brains need at least three examples before they begin to understand the procedure. As you work each problem, talk aloud so that students can hear you modeling the thought processes aloud and become more metacognitive.

**Adaptation:** Have students come to the dry-erase or SMART board or document camera and work math problems that can serve as visuals for the remainder of the class. Have them explain the steps in solving the problem so that students have an auditory link to the visual problem.

| | |
|---|---|
| **WHO:** | Elementary/Middle/High |
| **WHEN:** | After a lesson |
| **CONTENT AREA(S):** | Cross-curricular |

• Create a *word wall* by categorizing basic sight words and/or content-area vocabulary words and placing them on the wall under the appropriate alphabet letter or by the parts of speech they represent as they are taught.

**WHO:**                            Elementary/Middle/High
**WHEN:**                        During a lesson
**CONTENT AREA(S):**     Social studies

• During the course of the school year, add specific historical events to a timeline placed around the wall as they are taught so that students can visually see the relationships between sequential events in history.

## REFLECTION AND APPLICATION

> How will I incorporate *visuals* into
> instruction to engage students' brains?

**Which visuals am I already integrating as I teach the curriculum?**

**What additional visuals will I integrate?**

# Strategy 19

# Work Study and Apprenticeships

## WHAT: DEFINING THE STRATEGY

I had the privilege of conducting a workshop for the faculty of the Autry Technology Center in Enid, Oklahoma. Since I arrived early and had an opportunity to set up the technology for my presentation with time to spare, I took a guided tour of the facility. To say that I was impressed is an understatement! The facility houses approximately 300 high school students who spend part of their day in their local school and another part at the technology center. They are mixed in with adults who are high school graduates but are seeking real-world experience and a job. You see, by the time these students and adults finish the Autry Technology Center, they will have certification in a variety of careers such as dental hygienist, welder, cosmetologist, or graphic artist. I even have a personalized mouse pad that I will always treasure since it was created by the teacher and students in the graphic arts department.

Think back to when you finished high school. No doubt you can recall the names of many students in your senior class who did not have the grades or the SAT scores to place in the top 25th or even the 50th percentile of graduating seniors. However, fast-forward to your 10-year class reunion. How many of these so-called non-achievers became extremely successful in the actual world of work? Could it be that much of the knowledge and skill one acquires in school may have little relationship to the actual knowledge and skill required for success in real life? Could it be that for some occupations, on-the-job training may be infinitely more valuable than memorization and regurgitation of isolated facts, which seem to earn the *A*s in school? Students who may not be successful academically or who are discipline problems at their neighborhood schools appear to succeed at Autry and will graduate with a marketable skill that enables them to become employed immediately.

Work study, apprenticeships, practicums, and internships may be instructional strategies that afford students the best of both worlds: exposure in school to a wide variety of experiences that help students determine possible career choices and actual on-the-job work experiences that prepare students for success in the real world.

## WHY: THEORETICAL FRAMEWORK

To prepare students for their life after they have completed high school is the actual purpose of schooling (Sousa & Pilecki, 2013).

When students encounter experiential learning, they are led to higher levels of recall and retention (Sousa & Tomlinson, 2011).

An authentic social studies model accurately replicates the process of social studies research in the real world (Melber & Hunter, 2010).

One of the problems with high schools is their propensity to cover a great deal of content without providing students the opportunity to use that content in the context of authentic situations (Wiggins & McTighe, 2008).

Students should learn that mathematics is an ever-changing subject and that what we learn in school is related to the discoveries of real mathematicians and to everyday life (Rothstein, Rothstein, & Lauber, 2006).

When the learning is applicable to students' lives, students not only become more engaged but they also feel more responsible for finishing assignments and understand the relationship between their success in school and success in the real world (Algozzine et al., 2009b).

Students are motivated when teachers show them the connections between mastery in mathematics and their success in other subjects, as well as math's relevance in their daily lives (Posamentier & Jaye, 2006).

If high school or college graduates are to be successful in the workplace, they must possess three of the top applied skills of oral communication, teamwork/collaboration, and professionalism/work ethic (The Consortium, 2006).

Educated adults often have difficulty finding a job or meeting job expectations because large gaps can exist between the performance needed to be successful in a business setting and those required for school success (Sternberg & Grigorenko, 2000).

When students learn under the supervision of an expert in the field, they are given full participation in the process of learning and working (Wonacott, 1993).

Learning should be organized around cognitive-apprenticeship principles that stress subject-specific content and the skills required to function within the content (Berryman & Bailey, 1992).

When students observe and confer with an expert, they build technical skills and share tasks that relate those technical skills to their knowledge and interpretation (Wonacott, 1993).

# HOW: INSTRUCTIONAL ACTIVITIES

**WHO:** Middle/High
**WHEN:** Before a lesson
**CONTENT AREA(S):** Cross-curricular

• There are a number of different instruments that can assess a student's interest in and aptitude for a variety of professions. If the school does not already administer one to students, find one and allow students to take it so that they can begin to think about which professions they may like to pursue. I knew that I wanted to be a teacher at six years of age. I would line my dolls up in my bedroom and teach them for hours. Funny, I didn't have a single behavior problem!

**WHO:** Elementary/Middle/High
**WHEN:** Before or after a lesson
**CONTENT AREA(S):** Cross-curricular

• Familiarize students with the U.S. Secretary's Commission on Achieving Necessary Skills (SCANS, 1991), which delineates the five competencies and three foundational skills essential for high school graduates to possess if they were expected to be successful in the world of work in the year 2000. Even though this report was first issued in 1991, my daughter, Jessica, was asked to demonstrate six of them when she applied for and received a promotion to head chef of the banquet staff at the Ritz Carlton Hotel in Atlanta just a few months ago. The competencies and skills are as follows:

- o **Five Competencies:** Allocation of Resources, Interpersonal Skills, Information, Systems Thinking, and Technology
- o **Three Foundational Skills:** Basic Skills, Thinking Skills, and Personal Qualities

**WHO:** Elementary/Middle/High
**WHEN:** During a lesson
**CONTENT AREA(S):** Cross-curricular

• Initiate a career day in the school. Invite parents, scientists, historians, writers, mathematicians, dignitaries, local celebrities, radio station hosts, and other persons of interest to talk about their vocations and avocations. Have students research the careers in advance so that they are more knowledgeable and brainstorm pertinent questions to be asked during the visits. This career day can be done schoolwide or in an individual classroom.

**WHO:** Elementary/Middle/High
**WHEN:** After a lesson
**CONTENT AREA(S):** Cross-curricular

• As students complete various curricular objectives, invite professionals who use the given skills or knowledge in their daily jobs to speak to the class. For example, as math students complete a chapter on types of angles, have architects demonstrate to the class ways in which angles play a part in building bridges or houses. After these presentations, students are less likely to ask the question, *Why do we have to learn this?* Jessica, the chef at the Ritz Carlton, came to her sister Jennifer's second-grade class and talked about the importance of math in following recipes. They even made chocolate-covered pretzels during the presentation.

**WHO:**              Elementary/Middle/High
**WHEN:**             After a lesson
**CONTENT AREA(S):**  Cross-curricular

• Have students research professions of interest and create reports or projects to share what they have learned with the class. In this way, students get to glean information regarding an occupation of interest and can create a timeline of what specific schooling, job training, or apprenticeships would be required to fulfill that position. Students need to realize that, without adequate training and preparation, they will not awaken one day and occupy the position of a computer tech, teacher, doctor, lawyer, writer, or anything else.

**WHO:**              High
**WHEN:**             After a lesson
**CONTENT AREA(S):**  Cross-curricular

• Partner with local businesses who can make it possible for students to engage in internships, apprenticeships, and/or work-study projects either during the school year or during the summer months so that they can experience firsthand the knowledge and skills essential for the workplace. Allow them to spend time with professionals who use course content or skills in their daily occupations.

**WHO:**              Elementary/Middle/High
**WHEN:**             During a lesson
**CONTENT AREA(S):**  Cross-curricular

• Engage students in a service-learning project where they are providing a service for their school or community while mastering curricular objectives. For example, have them beautify the school grounds by planning and implementing a butterfly garden. Have them research the necessary components for the garden, perform the essential measurements of the grounds, and calculate what should be planted where while journaling the entire experience. Service learning is one of the best vehicles for combining character, interdisciplinary instruction, and real-world skills and strategies.

**WHO:**              Middle/High
**WHEN:**             Before, during, or after a lesson
**CONTENT AREA(S):**  Mathematics

• Have students adopt a local business and track its success or the lack of it over a specified time. Have students interview employees of the business in an effort to ascertain information about what product or service the business provides, what demands exist for the product, how the business supplies the product, and the current state of the business. Have students write about these experiences, and, based on research, make recommendations as to how the business could make changes to increase their revenue (Tate, 2014a).

**WHO:**      Elementary/Middle/High
**WHEN:**      During a lesson
**CONTENT AREA(S):**      Cross-curricular

• Take your students on a field trip to a job site related to the content you are teaching. For example, Warren Phillips, exemplary science teacher and co-author of the *Science Worksheets Don't Grow Dendrites* book, took his middle school students to Massachusetts Institute of Technology (MIT) annually where they could visit various science laboratories and talk to the scientists about their work. Following the trip, several of his students each year would decide that they wanted to be scientists or conduct laboratory work (Tate & Phillips, 2011).

**WHO:**      Middle/High
**WHEN:**      Before or after a lesson
**CONTENT AREA(S):**      Mathematics

• Under the direction of a teacher, have students plan and operate a school bank in which fellow students can deposit money. Use this real-life experience to enable students to master math concepts such as bank deposits and withdrawals, loans with interest rates, percentages, and so forth. Have students take turns serving as apprentices in the banking business.

**WHO:**      High
**WHEN:**      During a lesson
**CONTENT AREA(S):**      Cross-curricular

• Research school-to-work programs as a part of the School-to-Work Opportunities Act of 1994. This learning experience at an employer's work site includes all of the following elements:

  o a planned program of job training and work experience commensurate with a student's abilities;
  o a sequence of activities that increase in complexity and promote mastery of basic skills;
  o a learning experience that exposes the student to all aspects of an industry and promotes the development of transferable skills; and
  o a learning experience that provides for real or simulated tasks or assignments that causes students to develop higher-order thinking and problem-solving skills.

## REFLECTION AND APPLICATION

> ### How will I incorporate *work-study and apprenticeships* into instruction to engage students' brains?

Which work-study and apprenticeship activities am I already integrating as I teach the curriculum?

What additional activities will I integrate?

# Strategy 20

# Writing and Journals

## WHAT: DEFINING THE STRATEGY

With all the emphasis on technology, perhaps this chapter should be deleted, or the title, at the very least, changed to "Typing and Journals." Not so fast! Teachers ask this question of me a great deal, *What is more memorable to the brain—typing on a computer or writing in long hand?* Guess which one! If you said *writing*, you would be correct. Research (Longcamp et al., 2008; Sousa, 2007) appears to indicate that the things that we write down tend to stick to the brain better than the things we type on a computer. Have you ever written a list of groceries that you wanted to purchase at the store and then forgotten to take the list with you? Isn't it ironic that you can still recall the majority of items on the list? Therefore, there are times when we may prefer that our students write and other times when we want them typing. It simply depends on the purpose of the assignment and which is more appropriate for accomplishing that purpose.

A word of caution about writing: Many middle and high school teachers have students taking copious notes while they are lecturing. What's wrong with this picture? Since the brain can only pay conscious attention to one thing at a time, students are either attempting to write the notes and missing part of the lecture or attempting to listen to the lecture and missing many of the notes. Don't expect them to do both. I am not saying that you cannot multitask. I am saying that only one of those tasks is conscious. Everything else you are doing, you are doing unconsciously! If this is the case, what does it say about talking on the cell phone, or even texting, while driving? Very bad idea!

# WHY: THEORETICAL FRAMEWORK

Students stand a better chance of recognizing letters and characters, a skill necessary for reading, if they write the letters while they are being learned rather than typing them on the computer (Longcamp et al., 2008).

Students understand that notes are a work in progress and a valuable tool for memory when they have an opportunity to revise and review those notes (Dean et al., 2012).

Students should write the definitions of words they are attempting to remember in their own words since the brain tends to recall best those things that are personally relevant (Tileston, 2011).

In the largest study of writing programs, the researchers recommended that struggling writers be taught strategies for planning, revising, and editing their compositions (Graham & Perin, 2007).

The following framework should be adhered to when teaching students with learning disabilities to write: (1) providing students with a planning think sheet, (2) helping them create a first draft, and (3) incorporating a peer-coaching approach for revising and editing (Sousa, 2007).

When students were given written model solutions (examples that had been worked out) to refer to when solving math practice problems, they made fewer errors than a comparable group who solved a greater number of practice problems without the written model solutions (Posamentier & Jaye, 2006).

"Write to argue and persuade readers and write to convey information" are tied as the two most important types of writing required of incoming college students (ACT Inc., 2009).

If writers are to be prepared for college or career, they must know how to assert and defend claims, demonstrate their understanding on a subject, and convey what they are thinking, experiencing, imagining, or feeling (National Governors Association Center for Best Practices, Council of Chief State School Officers, 2010).

When the kinesthetic activity of writing is used to communicate math concepts, more neurons are engaged and students are made to organize their thoughts (Sousa, 2007).

Rubrics created and scored by students enable them to focus their writing and think more critically about it (Algozzine et al., 2009b).

Writing enables the brain to reverse the reading process. Rather than responding initially to external visual stimuli, during the writing process the brain starts with internal thoughts, chooses appropriate vocabulary to express those thoughts, and then produces the symbols for the words in writing (Wolfe & Nevills, 2004).

Having students write notes or copy them from the board while the teacher continues talking can be a distraction (Jensen & Nickelsen, 2008).

# HOW: INSTRUCTIONAL ACTIVITIES

**WHO:** Elementary/Middle
**WHEN:** During a lesson
**CONTENT AREA(S):** Cross-curricular

- Engage students in a prewriting activity called *four square writing* according to the following guidelines:

  o Take a piece of 8- by 11-inch white paper and fold it both vertically and horizontally so that when you open it, the paper forms four squares.
  o Draw a rectangle in the middle of the paper and label it with a small *Box 1*. Box 1 would contain a topic sentence for a paragraph to be written.
  o Label the top left square as *Box 2*, the top right square as *Box 3*, the bottom left square as *Box 4*, and the bottom right square as *Box 5*.
  o Boxes 2–4 would each contain one detail or reason in support of the topic sentence in box 1. Additional sentences could be written in boxes 2–4 in support of the details already recorded in each box.
  o Box 5 would contain either a conclusion, summary, or feeling statement in support of the topic sentence.
  o From this prewriting activity, students can then form paragraphs. Students in kindergarten who are not yet writing can draw pictures in each box or dictate their sentences to the teacher who can then record them (Tate, 2014a, pp. 154–155).

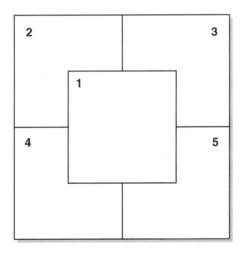

**Figure 20.1**

**WHO:** Elementary/Middle/High
**WHEN:** During a lesson
**CONTENT AREA(S):** Cross-curricular

- As you present a lecturette (a mini-lecture of five to seven minutes), have students write key concepts and phrases that will help them remember your content. Be sure to give them time to write so that their brains will not have to engage in two behaviors simultaneously—listening to your continued talk and trying to remember what to write.

| | |
|---|---|
| **WHO:** | Elementary/Middle/High |
| **WHEN:** | During a lesson |
| **CONTENT AREA(S):** | Cross-curricular |

• Give students many opportunities to write for a variety of real-world, cross-curricular purposes. Reasons for writing should proceed naturally during instruction and include the following: to persuade, to inform, to express, and to entertain (PIE). For example, have students write an essay about one event that changed the course of their lives. Watch the emotional reaction that this activity can engender! Then use their essays to teach them about the writing process in language arts.

| | |
|---|---|
| **WHO:** | Elementary/Middle/High |
| **WHEN:** | During a lesson |
| **CONTENT AREA(S):** | Cross-curricular |

• Give students a variety of media that provide them with opportunities to express their ideas in writing. These could include, but not be limited to, posters, brochures, scripts for plays, book jackets, commercials, and graphic organizers. Consult Strategy 5 ("Graphic Organizers, Semantic Maps, and Word Webs") for examples of various mind maps.

| | |
|---|---|
| **WHO:** | Elementary/Middle/High |
| **WHEN:** | During a lesson |
| **CONTENT AREA(S):** | Language arts |

• Expand students' reading and writing vocabularies by identifying "tired words" that are overused in students' writing, such as said, like, good, and pretty. Have students brainstorm a list of synonyms that give them alternative vocabulary words to make their writing more interesting and appealing. For example, for the word "said," the brainstormed list could include "replied," "exclaimed," "declared," "responded," and "stated." Compile a class list of alternative words and post it on the wall for students to use during future writing assignments. If students cannot think of alternative words, appoint a resident thesaurian, a student who possesses the thesaurus and can provide more rigorous vocabulary words. Forbid students from using the tired words and have them incorporate the new words appropriately into their writing.

| | |
|---|---|
| **WHO:** | Elementary/Middle/High |
| **WHEN:** | During a lesson |
| **CONTENT AREA(S):** | Mathematics |

• Have students keep math journals in which they could write the steps when solving computational or word problems. Not only will the written steps assist the student in remembering the sequence of the solution, but it will also provide insight to the teacher into the thinking of the student during problem solving.

| | |
|---|---|
| **WHO:** | Elementary/Middle/High |
| **WHEN:** | During a lesson |
| **CONTENT AREA(S):** | Cross-curricular |

• Incorporate *Quick Writes* throughout a lesson. Stop periodically during the lesson and have students write a concept just taught. Writing, even for a minute, will help to reinforce the content. For example, stop your lesson and have students do the following: *Write the steps in the scientific process. Write the three causes of the Civil War.*

| | |
|---|---|
| **WHO:** | Elementary/Middle/High |
| **WHEN:** | During a lesson |
| **CONTENT AREA(S):** | Cross-curricular |

• Have students carry a piece of writing through the following five stages of the writing process for publication in a class book.

- o **Prewriting**—Have students brainstorm a jot list of ideas regarding an original composition or related to an assigned topic.
- o **Writing**—Have students write a rough draft of the composition according to teacher guidelines.
- o **Editing**—Have students assess one another's writing according to a rubric developed by the class.
- o **Revising**—Have students revise their composition in light of peer feedback from the rubric.
- o **Final Draft**—Have students produce a written or typed final draft that is ready for publication in the class book.

| | |
|---|---|
| **WHO:** | Elementary/Middle/High |
| **WHEN:** | During a lesson |
| **CONTENT AREA(S):** | Cross-curricular |

• In an effort to improve the students' quality of journal writing, have them brainstorm an *alphabet book* that would include vocabulary chunked according to the letters of the alphabet, yet pertinent to a unit of study. For example, during a unit of geometry, a *geometry alphabet book* could look like the following: *acute, base, circumference, diameter, equilateral, figure,* and so forth. Post these words as a visual or have students include them in their notebooks for ready reference.

| | |
|---|---|
| **WHO:** | Elementary/Middle/High |
| **WHEN:** | After a lesson |
| **CONTENT AREA(S):** | Cross-curricular |

• Following a unit of study in any content area, have students record their thoughts regarding the unit in their personal journals. The following open-ended question starters may serve to spark the thinking of students:

- State at least three major concepts you learned in this unit.
- What was your favorite activity in which the class participated?
- What was your least favorite activity in which the class participated?
- How can you apply what you have learned to your personal life or to a future career choice?
- If this unit were taught again, what things would you change?

**WHO:**                     Elementary/Middle/High
**WHEN:**                    Before or after a lesson
**CONTENT AREA(S):**         Cross-curricular

• Provide time daily for students to write in a personal journal regarding topics of choice, including descriptions of incidents that have happened at home, personal reflections on class assignments, or feeling or emotions expressed. Journals are not graded and students can indicate whether they want their entries read by the teacher by leaving the page unfolded if it is to be read or folding the page lengthwise if it is not to be read.

## REFLECTION AND APPLICATION

How will I incorporate *writing and journals* into instruction to engage students' brains?

**Which writing and journal activities am I already integrating as I teach the curriculum?**

**What additional activities will I integrate?**

# Resource A

## *Brain-Compatible Lesson Plan*

In this third edition of the original bestseller, a brain-compatible lesson plan continues to serve as a resource since teachers have found it very helpful as they work to include the 20 instructional strategies into their lesson design. In fact, an adaptation of this plan is currently being used nationwide as school systems revise curriculum and ensure that teachers are planning lessons that not only maximize student achievement and help students meet content standards but also go a long way toward enabling students to retain content long after the examinations are over. It answers the following essential question: *How can I incorporate the 20 brain-compatible strategies into my daily lesson plans so that students will understand and remember the content?* The sample lesson plan is displayed on page 201.

It does not matter whether you use this particular lesson plan template as you put your lessons together. In fact, a lengthy written response to each question would be very time consuming. You may even have your own unique lesson plan design, and it is not necessary to change from the form that you are currently using. What does matter is whether you can honestly ask and answer the five questions on the plan that are delineated in the paragraphs that follow.

## SECTION 1: LESSON OBJECTIVE: WHAT DO YOU WANT YOUR STUDENTS TO KNOW AND BE ABLE TO DO?

The first essential question of Section 1 has changed since the original lesson plan was developed. As a teacher of the *7 Habits of Highly Effective People* (Covey, 1996), it makes sense that all lessons should *Begin with the End in Mind* (Habit 2). Obviously, when teachers are planning lessons, the first question they should ask themselves should be, *What do I want students to know and/or be able to do by the time the lesson is completed?*

As I travel the United States, many teachers are telling me that they know that they should incorporate the brain-compatible strategies during instruction, but they simply do not have the time. Teachers express their frustration at being asked to teach more and more content every year in the same amount of time with nothing being eliminated.

For example, an American History teacher told me that his curriculum expects him to cover the Vietnam War in one day. How in the world can you teach such an important war in one class period? I empathized with his plight but I wanted to tell him what a famous educator, Madeline Hunter, said years ago. She related that if all teachers are doing is covering content, then they should get a shovel and cover it with dirt since it is dead to memory as far as the brain is concerned. The question should be: *What do you want your students to know regarding the Vietnam War?*

During my international travels and teaching in other countries, many of whom outscore us on tests of achievement, *less appears to be more*. Their textbooks are about one-third the size of ours and content is chunked together into relevant concepts to be taught. Why can't we in the United States look at our content that way? The Common Core State Standards appear to be a step in the right direction since the standards limit the number of specific objectives that teachers need to teach annually.

I also pray that the days are gone when teachers are dependent on their textbooks. They have students open the textbook to page one at the beginning of the school year and conclude instruction with the last page of the book prior to summer vacation. The days should be over when teaching content consists solely of round-robin oral reading the chapter as the class follows along in their textbooks and then having the class answer the questions at the end of the chapter. Content may be covered but retention is compromised. In order to answer the essential question regarding the Vietnam War, the textbook may not even be necessary!

A better way of teaching calls for a paradigm shift on the part of many professionals who look at their subject matter as content to be covered or isolated skills to be mastered. Instead, the question should be, *What should my students be responsible for knowing or doing by the end of the lesson?*

Let's look again at Scenario II in the Introduction of this text. When I taught *Antigone*, Scene 3, students needed to be able to make inferences regarding both the structure and elements of drama.

## SECTION 2: ASSESSMENT: HOW WILL YOU KNOW THAT STUDENTS HAVE MASTERED ESSENTIAL LEARNING?

When planning a lesson, if you wait until the completion of the plan to decide how you will assess your students, you have actually waited too long. I can still visualize myself as a student in school. I remember being stressed on test days because assessment sometimes meant trying to guess what my teachers were going to put on their tests. If I guessed correctly, I would manage to make an *A*. However, if I guessed incorrectly, even if I studied feverishly, my grade was not so good. The current research tells us to tell students what you expect. Your expectations should not be kept a secret. Tell students what they should know and be able to do at the culmination of a lesson or unit of study. In this way, your assessment may be a challenge to the brains of students, but never a high stressor or threat. Consider this analogy: How can a pilot file a flight plan without knowing the destination? Tell students their destination, and they will stand a better chance of arriving there.

In the lesson on Scene 3 of *Antigone*, inferential questioning during partner and whole-group discussion, as well as written responses, would provide some formative assessment regarding students' abilities to make inferences about the structure and elements of drama.

## SECTION 3: WAYS TO GAIN/MAINTAIN ATTENTION: HOW WILL YOU GAIN AND MAINTAIN STUDENTS' ATTENTION?

(Consider need, novelty, meaning, and emotion.)

"This isn't a good time. I'm in trouble with the Dean for using a cell phone in class. I'll call you back."

SOURCE: Bacall (2003a).

There is so much stimuli in the environment that brains are very particular regarding what they choose to pay attention to. When you are teaching, you are vying for that attention. But your lesson may be competing with a text message from their smartphone, a conversation with a peer, a noise in the hall, a colorful leaf on a tree outside the window, or reflections of an argument that the student had with his parent before he came to school. Students can even be staring you in the face and not paying a bit of attention to what you are teaching.

There is also a structure in the brain called the hippocampus that pretty much determines whether a lesson will be remembered. If the hippocampi of your students determine that your lesson is not worth remembering, then when your students fall asleep at night, the delete button of the brain is pushed and your lesson ends up in the trash. Let me tell you one way you can tell that your lesson was deleted: Your students return the next day and, when you review, it is like they were not present when the information was taught. Either the lesson never entered the brain or it was deleted while students slept!

Good news! There are four major ways to gain and maintain your students' attention. I had the benefit of using all four ways in my lesson. Do you have to grab students' attention using all four ways in every lesson you teach? Absolutely not! Do you have to grab students' attention using at least one way? Absolutely so! The ways are *need, novelty, meaning,* and *emotion.*

## Need

The first way to grab the attention of your students is through need. When students do not see the need for learning what you are teaching, they just may not pay attention. If students see the purpose in what you are teaching, they will see the need to learn it. For example, I did not see the need to memorize the phone numbers of my three children. Each number was programmed into my cell phone. However while traveling, my phone malfunctioned and I could not retrieve anyone's number. I could have easily asked to borrow the phone of another person for an important call to my pregnant daughter, but I truly did not know her number. Even in this age of technology, there are some things that we need to keep hidden in our brains for immediate retrieval.

When students see the purpose for your lesson, they will see the need to learn the content. Simply telling them that they will need the information for a subsequent test may not be enough motivation for many students. Some couldn't care less! In our sample lesson, I gave students a purpose. As literate citizens who are ready for college or career, we will be reading the genre of drama. All of our understanding of that text will not be literally stated. There are times when we need to *read between the lines.* This involves our ability to infer, which grows our brain cells.

## Novelty

Sometimes need is simply not sufficient for engaging students in the lesson. You may know that your students need the information but your students don't share your sense of urgency. The good news is that you have three more ways to gain their attention. A second way is by teaching your content in a novel or interesting way. The brain tends to pay attention to things in the environment that are new or different. As I stated earlier, I pay no attention to the initial flight instructions when I am on an airplane. I know I should, but I have heard it so many times that I could actually recite it myself. In my workshops, I actually show people where the exits are, like they do in the visual. There are a few exceptions. Some Southwest Airlines flight attendants and the new Delta videos give the flight instructions using the strategy of humor. Whatever I am doing at the time when this happens, I stop and pay attention. Why? Because the instructions are presented in a new and different way.

While you certainly want consistency in your class rituals and procedures, you will want to vary your lesson delivery. When you change your location in the room, your voice inflection, or the strategies you use to deliver your lesson, you are being novel, and you stand a better chance of gaining and maintaining your students' attention. Providing them with the same sets of worksheets or a similar lecture just won't hold the attention of most students.

The 20 strategies provide you with many ways to be novel. Think of all the novel stories you and your students can tell, the variety of songs you can play, the projects in which you can engage your students, and all the different movements you can use to put information into procedural memory. Although there are only 20 strategies, the use of those strategies for novel lessons is endless!

In our sample lesson, I used a number of different instructional strategies to engage students in the lesson and it worked! Not one student appeared to be off task during the entire period.

## Meaning

Because the brain's purpose is survival in the real world, when you are connecting your content to real life, you are making it meaningful. When you are not, students will raise their hands and ask this question: *Why do we have to learn this?* As I teach, I take every opportunity to use real-life examples to illustrate my points. When I tell students the true story about the fact that my father had the trait for sickle-cell anemia and how that trait has been passed on to my sister and her daughter, that story goes a long way toward giving my science lesson on dominant and recessive genes more meaning. When teachers have students write about one decision that they made that changed the course of their lives, the writing lesson becomes unforgettable! Even mathematics isn't a scary and abstract mystery when everyday life applications are used to teach it (Posamentier & Jaye, 2006).

It was very meaningful in the lesson when we first looked at the elements of some dramas on television, such as *The Real Housewives of Atlanta* or compared Creon's view of women to men's view of women today.

## Emotion

Of all the ways to gain and maintain students' attention, emotion may be the most powerful! Emotion places experiences in reflexive memory, one of the strongest memory systems in the brain and helps to ensure retention. In fact, you will not soon forget anything that happened to you in your personal life or in the world at large that was emotional. I bet you can even remember where you were when it happened. For example, where were you on January 28, 1986, when you were informed that the *Challenger* had exploded? We lost seven astronauts that day, including a teacher by the name of Christa McAuliffe.

You do not, however, want to use a negative definition of emotion when talking about teaching and learning. If you were ever in the classroom of a teacher you did not like, you will never forget being in that teacher's room. Those memories stay with you. However, chances are you will not remember the content that the teacher taught. While you were sitting there, your brain was in survival mode, and when the brain is under threat only information crucial to survival is recalled.

Teachers who are emotional about their content are passionate and enthusiastic! No doubt, you remember a math teacher who influenced you to love math or a science teacher whose hands-on lessons were unforgettable! How can we expect students to become excited about our content if we are not excited about our content?

In our lesson, even though Sophocles can be difficult to understand and often thought of as boring, we made it fun and motivating by the dramatic way in which students came to the front of the room and read their lines and the conversations about today's dramas and how they differed from the days of Sophocles. *Antigone* itself is filled with drama since so many of the characters lead tragic lives that ended in death. The lesson was highly engaging and the positive emotion throughout was obvious.

*Need, novelty, meaning,* and *emotion* are four ways to gain the brain's attention. You do not need to have all four working for you in one lesson. Even one, used appropriately, will work as you compete with the multitude of stimuli surrounding your students during your lesson presentation.

## SECTION 4: CONTENT CHUNKS: HOW WILL YOU DIVIDE AND TEACH THE CONTENT TO ENGAGE STUDENTS' BRAINS?

Many years ago, a guru in the field of education by the name of Madeline Hunter asked another question: *How do you eat an elephant?* The answer, of course, was *one bite at a time.* The adult brain can only hold approximately seven bits of information (plus or minus two) simultaneously, which is why so much in the real world comes in a series of seven. There are seven days in a week, numbers in a phone number minus the area code, colors in the rainbow, notes on the scale, wonders of the ancient world, continents, *Habits of Highly Effective People* and dwarfs, to name a few. The way to get the brain to remember more than seven isolated bits would be to connect or chunk those bits together. This is why the Social Security number, which is more than seven digits, is in chunks. It is nine digits and, therefore, needs to be connected together into three chunks. A telephone number with an area code is 10 digits. However, it is also divided into three chunks to make it easier for you to remember. You see, the brain remembers a chunk as if it were one piece of information, rather than separate numbers.

Your job is to determine how many chunks or lesson segments are needed for you to get across the objective to your students. The chunking for a class of gifted students may be different from a group of students in remedial reading. Just determine how much your students' brains can hold at one time.

I have added another question to Madeline Hunter's original question: *How do you digest an elephant?* The answer, of course, is that you have to *chew it up*. Activity enables the brain to *chew up* information. Chew is a metaphor for the fact that the activity embedded in each chunk enables the brain to process or *digest* what it is learning. A classroom where there is little opportunity for students to process what they are learning is a classroom where students are not performing at optimal levels and may not be comprehending or retaining much at all.

In the sample lesson, I was able to teach the lesson using only one chunk or lesson segment. I did, however, incorporate a number of different activities for processing that one concept.

## SECTION 5: BRAIN-COMPATIBLE STRATEGIES: WHICH WILL YOU USE TO DELIVER CONTENT?

By the time a teacher completes a lesson plan, the activities included in the lesson should reflect the 20 brain-compatible strategies outlined in this book. In fact, on the bottom of the sample lesson-plan template, all 20 strategies are listed so that teachers have a ready reference for their use.

In every lesson I teach, regardless of which grade level or content area, I attempt to incorporate at least four of the strategies, one from each of the four modalities—visual, auditory, kinesthetic, and tactile—knowing that I probably have all four modalities represented in that class. (Refer to Figure 0.1 in the Introduction for a correlation of the strategies to the learning modalities.) In this way, regardless of student preferences, there is an activity in the lesson for every student and instruction can be differentiated based on students' learning needs.

In our sample lesson, strategies that were used to teach the objective included the following: (1) a partner discussion on Scenes 1 and 2 of *Antigone*, (2) a whole-class discussion on the review of the elements of drama, (3) eight different students role playing the parts of Creon and Haemon, (4) all students standing (movement) as they read the part of the Choragus, (5) laughter (humor) throughout, and (6) students writing the answers to some assigned inference questions.

Following the blank lesson-plan template, you will find three cross-curricular sample lessons that I have actually taught to students—a second-grade mathematics lesson, a seventh-grade lesson, and a high school World History lesson. If you come to the end of a planned lesson and have not utilized any of the brain-compatible strategies, you will need to go back and plan it again. It is not a brain-compatible lesson and will probably not be remembered by your students! No one is asking you to teach **harder**. Teaching is difficult business! I know first-hand since I, along with my daughter, Jennifer; sister, Ann; and niece, Erica are all teachers. I am suggesting that you teach **smarter**! In summary, teaching smarter means the following:

- **identifying what you want students to know and be able to do and telling them what that is at the beginning of the lesson;**
- **determining how you will know when students have mastered that essential learning;**
- **deciding how you will gain and maintain students' attention throughout the lesson;**
- **figuring out how many different lesson segments (chunks) are necessary to teach the objective; and**
- **integrating the appropriate instructional strategies into each chunk.**

# BRAIN-COMPATIBLE LESSON PLAN

**Lesson Objective(s):** *What do you want students to know and be able to do?*

**Assessment (Traditional/Authentic):** *How will you know students have mastered essential learning?*

---

**Ways to Gain/Maintain Attention (Primacy):** *How will you gain and maintain students' attention? Consider need, novelty, meaning, or emotion.*

---

**Content Chunks:** *How will you divide and teach the content to engage students' brains?*

**Lesson Segment 1:**

**Activities:**

**Lesson Segment 2:**

**Activities:**

**Lesson Segment 3:**

**Activities:**

---

**Brain-Compatible Strategies:** Which will you use to deliver content?

- ☐ Brainstorming/Discussion
- ☐ Drawing/Artwork
- ☐ Field Trips
- ☐ Games
- ☐ Graphic Organizers/Semantic Maps/Word Webs
- ☐ Humor
- ☐ Manipulatives/Experiments/Labs/Models
- ☐ Metaphors/Analogies/Similes
- ☐ Mnemonic Devices
- ☐ Movement

- ☐ Music/Rhythm/Rhyme/Rap
- ☐ Project/Problem-Based Learning
- ☐ Reciprocal Teaching/Cooperative Learning
- ☐ Role Plays/Drama/Pantomimes/Charades
- ☐ Storytelling
- ☐ Technology
- ☐ Visualization/Guided Imagery
- ☐ Visuals
- ☐ Work Study/Apprenticeships
- ☐ Writing/Journals

# BRAIN-COMPATIBLE LESSON PLAN

## Second-Grade Math

**Lesson Objective(s):** *What do you want students to know and be able to do?*

Use standard, word, and expanded forms to represent numbers up to 1,200.

**Assessment (Traditional/Authentic):** *How will you know students have mastered essential learning?*

Use place-value blocks to show a given number.

---

**Ways to Gain/Maintain Attention (Primacy):** *How will you gain and maintain students' attention? Consider need, novelty, meaning, or emotion.*

Why do you need to know place value?

---

**Content Chunks:** *How will you divide and teach the content to engage students' brains?*

**Lesson Segment 1:** Reading numbers aloud

**Activities:** Have students take turns standing in line to show appropriate place value.

**Lesson Segment 2:** Showing the value of each position

**Activities:** Work with a partner and place-value blocks to show given numbers.

**Lesson Segment 3:**

**Activities:**

---

**Brain-Compatible Strategies:** *Which will you use to deliver content?*

- ☒ Brainstorming/Discussion
- ☐ Drawing/Artwork
- ☐ Field Trips
- ☐ Games
- ☐ Graphic Organizers/Semantic Maps/Word Webs
- ☐ Humor
- ☒ Manipulatives/Experiments/ Labs/Models
- ☐ Metaphors/Analogies/Similes
- ☐ Mnemonic Devices
- ☒ Movement

- ☐ Music/Rhythm/Rhyme/Rap
- ☐ Project/Problem-Based Learning
- ☒ Reciprocal Teaching/Cooperative Learning
- ☐ Role Plays//Drama/Pantomimes/ Charades
- ☐ Storytelling
- ☐ Technology
- ☐ Visualization/Guided Imagery
- ☒ Visuals
- ☐ Work Study/Apprenticeships
- ☐ Writing/Journals

# BRAIN-COMPATIBLE LESSON PLAN

## Seventh-Grade English

**Lesson Objective(s):** *What do you want students to know and be able to do?*

Students will define four rhetorical fallacies and categorize 15 statements in terms of the fallacy they exemplify.

**Assessment (Traditional/Authentic):** *How will you know students have mastered essential learning?*

Volunteers and nonvolunteers will answer questions defining types of fallacies and place 15 statements into the correct column according to the persuasive technique that they exemplify.

---

**Ways to Gain/Maintain Attention (Primacy):** *How will you gain and maintain students' attention? Consider need, novelty, meaning, or emotion.*

Use meaningful, real-life examples to show how advertisers use persuasive techniques to convince an audience to choose their products.

---

**Content Chunks:** *How will you divide and teach the content to engage students' brains?*

**Lesson Segment 1:** Define types of rhetorical fallacies and categorize examples.

**Activities:** Whole-class discussion of types of fallacies and categorizing fallacies with a partner; individual writing examples of each type of fallacy.

**Lesson Segment 2:**

**Activities:**

**Lesson Segment 3:**

**Activities:**

---

**Brain-Compatible Strategies:** *Which will you use to deliver content?*

- ☒ Brainstorming/Discussion
- ☐ Drawing/Artwork
- ☐ Field Trips
- ☐ Games
- ☐ Graphic Organizers/Semantic Maps/Word Webs
- ☒ Humor
- ☐ Manipulatives/Experiments/ Labs/Models
- ☒ Metaphors/Analogies/Similes
- ☐ Mnemonic Devices
- ☐ Movement

- ☐ Music/Rhythm/Rhyme/Rap
- ☐ Project/Problem-Based Learning
- ☒ Reciprocal Teaching/Cooperative Learning
- ☐ Role Plays/Drama/Pantomimes/ Charades
- ☐ Storytelling
- ☐ Technology
- ☐ Visualization/Guided Imagery
- ☒ Visuals
- ☐ Work Study/Apprenticeships
- ☒ Writing/Journals

# BRAIN-COMPATIBLE LESSON PLAN

## Tenth-Grade World History

**Lesson Objective(s):** *What do you want students to know and be able to do?*

Compare and contrast the power, citizenship, government, culture, and society of the city-states Athens and Sparta.

**Assessment (Traditional/Authentic):** *How will you know students have mastered essential learning?*

Graphic organizers should reflect similarities and differences.

---

**Ways to Gain/Maintain Attention (Primacy):** *How will you gain and maintain students' attention? Consider need, novelty, meaning, or emotion.*

Where would you rather reside, Athens or Sparta? Why?

---

**Content Chunks:** *How will you divide and teach the content to engage students' brains?*

**Lesson Segment 1:** Compare/contrast Athens and Sparta.

**Activities:** Work in groups to complete the Venn diagram regarding one aspect of each citi-state.

Present to class.
Complete advertising poster for Athens or Sparta.

**Lesson Segment 2:**

**Activities:**

**Lesson Segment 3:**

**Activities:**

---

**Brain-Compatible Strategies:** *Which will you use to deliver content?*

- ☒ Brainstorming/Discussion
- ☒ Drawing/Artwork
- ☐ Field Trips
- ☐ Games
- ☒ Graphic Organizers/Semantic Maps/Word Webs
- ☐ Humor
- ☐ Manipulatives/Experiments/Labs/Models
- ☐ Metaphors/Analogies/Similes
- ☐ Mnemonic Devices
- ☐ Movement
- ☐ Music/Rhythm/Rhyme/Rap
- ☐ Project/Problem-Based Learning
- ☒ Reciprocal Teaching/Cooperative Learning
- ☐ Role Plays/Drama/Pantomimes/Charades
- ☐ Storytelling
- ☐ Technology
- ☐ Visualization/Guided Imagery
- ☒ Visuals
- ☐ Work Study/Apprenticeships
- ☐ Writing/Journals

# Resource B

*Graphic Organizers*

# Character Traits

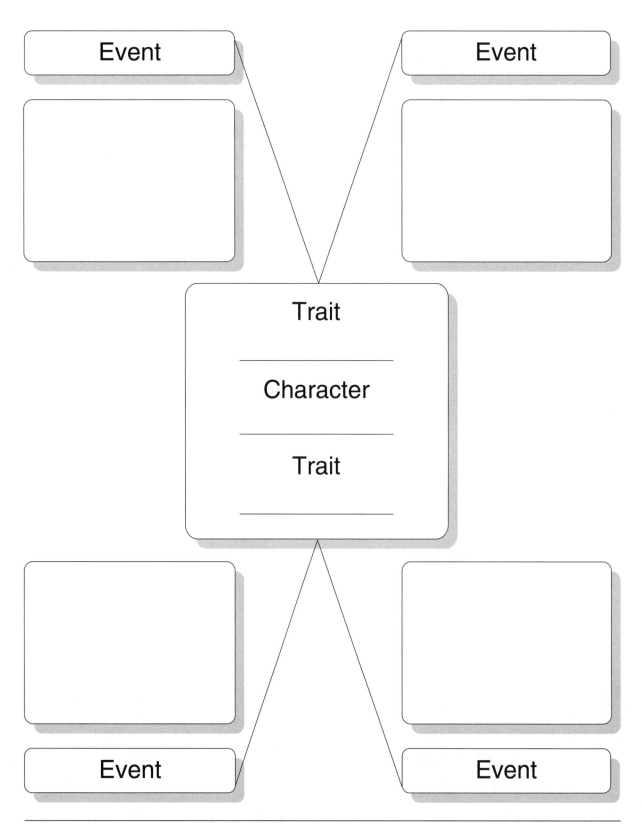

Event

Event

Trait

_____

Character

_____

Trait

_____

Event

Event

# The K-N-L Strategy

Topic: _____

| What I Know | What I Need to Know | What I Learned |
|---|---|---|
| | | |
| | | |
| | | |
| | | |
| | | |
| | | |
| | | |
| | | |
| | | |

# Vocabulary Word Web

# Story Map

Title     _____

Setting

Characters     _____     _____

_____     _____

_____     _____

Problem

Event 1     _____

Event 2     _____

Event 3     _____

Event 4     _____

Solution

# "5Ws and an H"

Use the organizer below to create a "5Ws and an H" summary.

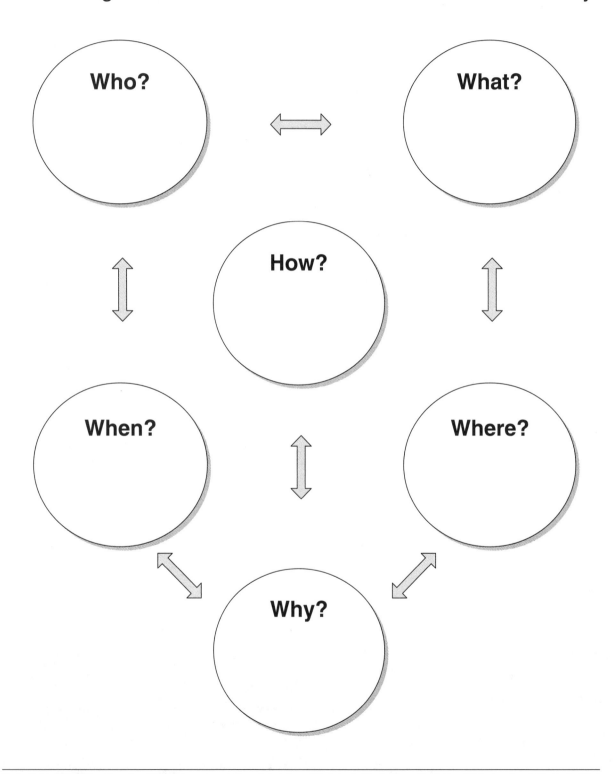

# Cause/Effect Organizer

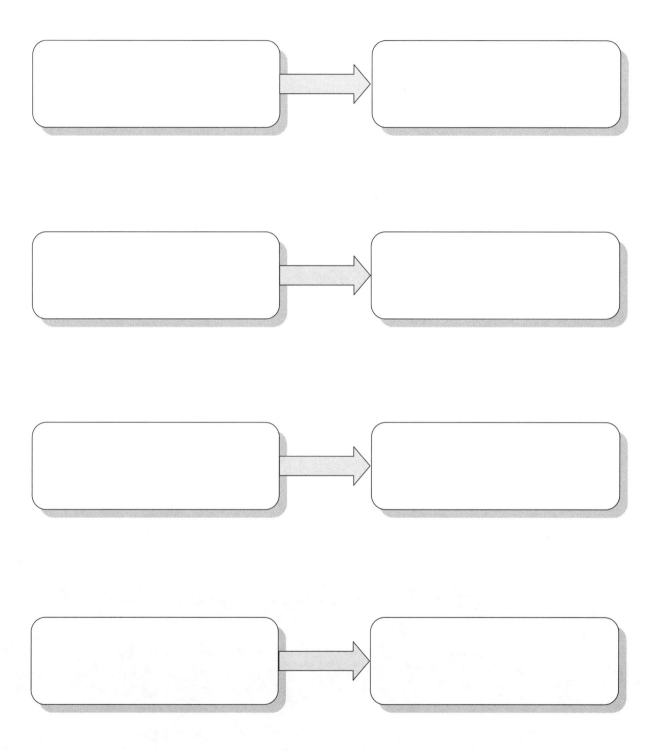

# Comparison Organizer

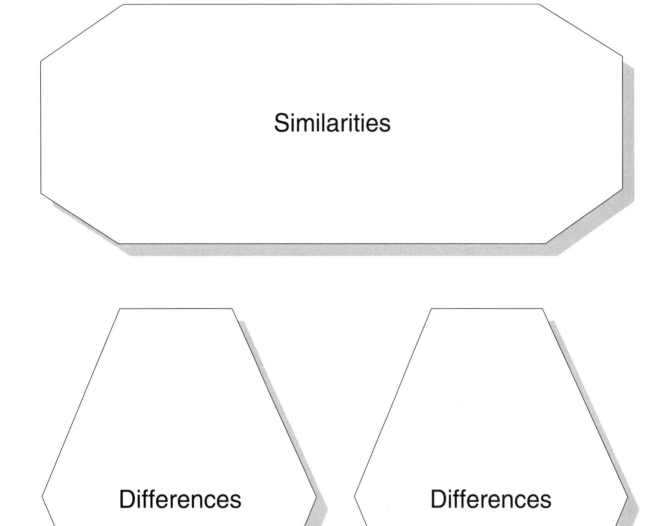

# Cycle Organizer

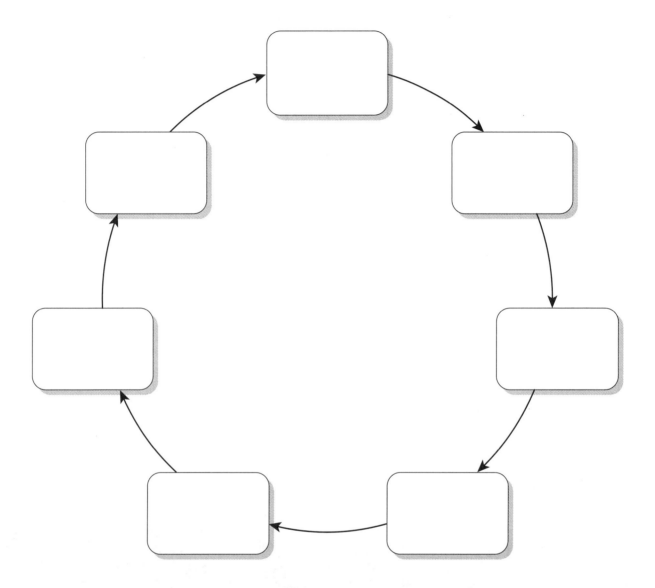

# Sequence Organizer

First

Second

Third

Fourth

Fifth

Sixth

# Topic Description Organizer

# Problem/Solution Organizer

| Problem | Solution | Effect |
|---|---|---|
| | | |
| | | |
| | | |
| | | |
| | | |
| | | |
| | | |
| | | |
| | | |
| | | |
| | | |
| | | |

216

# Compare/Contrast Organizer

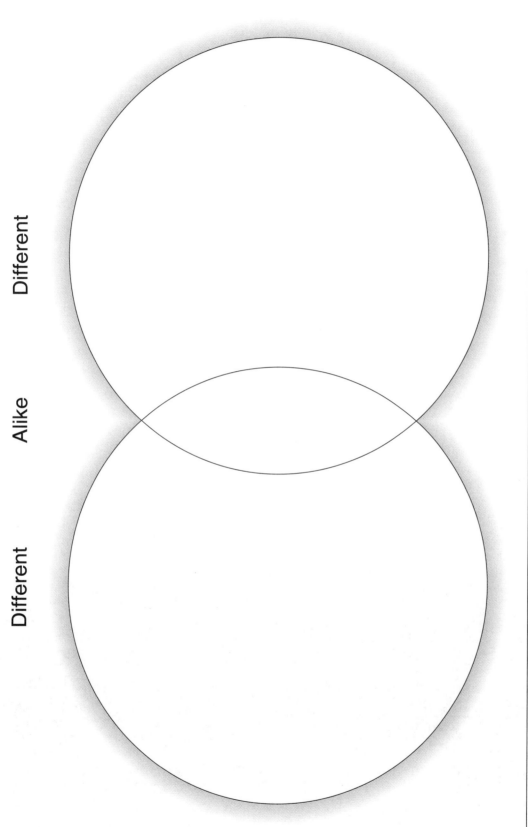

Different     Alike     Different

# Mind Map

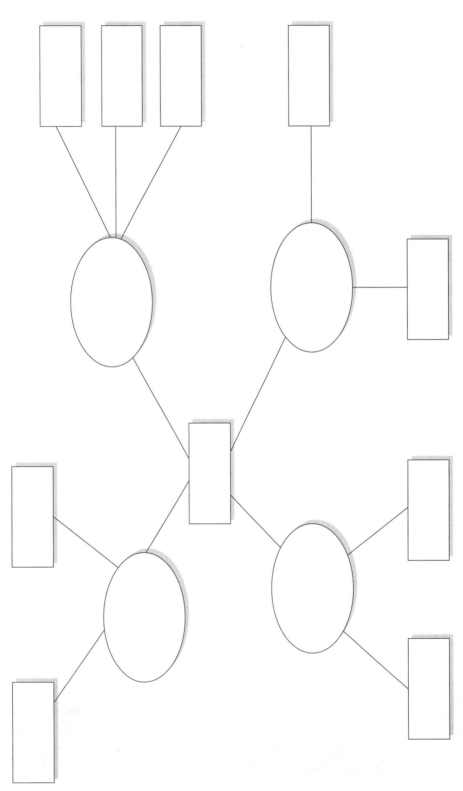

# Bibliography

Access Center. (2004, October 1). Retrieved August 31, 2009, from http://coe. jme.edu/mathvidsr/disabilities.htm.

ACT, Inc. (2009). *ACT National Curriculum Survey 2009.* Retrieved March 5, 2015, from www.act.org/research/policymakers/pdf/National Curriculum Survey2009.pdf.

Algozzine, B., Campbell, P., & Wang, A. (2009a). *63 tactics for teaching diverse learners: Grades K–6.* Thousand Oaks, CA: Corwin.

Algozzine, B., Campbell, P., & Wang, A. (2009b). *63 tactics for teaching diverse learners: Grades 6–12.* Thousand Oaks, CA: Corwin.

Allen, R. (2008). *Green light classrooms: Teaching techniques that accelerate learning.* Victoria, Australia: Hawker Brownlow.

Allen, R., & Currie, J. (2012). *U-turn teaching: Strategies to accelerate learning and transform middle school achievement.* Thousand Oaks, CA: Corwin.

Allen, R., & Scozzi, N. (2012). *Sparking student synapses 9–12: Think critically and accelerate learning.* Thousand Oaks, CA: Corwin.

Allen, R., & Wood, W. W. (2013). *The rock'n'roll classroom: Using music to manage mood, energy, and learning.* Thousand Oaks, CA: Corwin.

Bacall, A. (2003a). *The lighter side of teaching.* Thousand Oaks, CA: Corwin.

Bacall, A. (2003b). *The lighter side of technology in education.* Thousand Oaks, CA: Corwin.

Barell, J. (2010). Problem-based learning: The foundation for 21st century skills. In J. Bellanca & R. Brandt (Eds.), *21st century skills: Rethinking how students learn.* Bloomington, IN: Solution Tree Press.

Barr, R. D., & Parrett, W. (2007). *Saving our students, saving our schools: 50 proven strategies for helping.* Thousand Oaks, CA: Corwin.

Bellanca, J. A., Fogarty, R. J., & Pete, B. M. (2012). *How to teach thinking skills within the common core: 7 key student proficiencies of the new national standards.* Bloomington, IN: Solution Tree Press.

Bender, W. (2005). *Differentiating math instruction: Strategies that work for K–8 classrooms!* Thousand Oaks, CA: Corwin.

Bender, W. N. (2012). *RTI in middle and high schools.* Bloomington, IN: Solution Tree Press.

Berman, S. (2008). *Thinking strategies for science: Grades 5–12* (2nd ed.). Victoria, Australia: Hawker Brownlow.

Berryman, S. E., & Bailey, T. R. (1992). *The double helix of education and the economy.* New York: Institute on Education and the Economy, Columbia University Teachers College.

Bloom, B. S. (Ed.). (1956). *Taxonomy of educational objectives. The classification of educational goals, by a committee of college and university examiners.* New York: Longmans.

Bulla, D. (1996). *Think math! Interactive loops for groups.* Chicago: Zephyr Press.

Burgess, R. (2000). *Laughing lessons: 1492/3 ways to make teaching and learning fun.* Minneapolis, MN: Free Spirit.

Burke, K. (2009). *How to assess authentic learning* (5th ed.). Thousand Oaks, CA: Corwin.

Busche, L. (2013). *Handsketching: Things you didn't know your doodles could accomplish.* Retrieved March 4, 2015, www.smashingmagazines.com/.../things-y.

Caine, R. N., Caine, G., McClintic, C., & Klimek, K. (2005). *12 brain/mind learning principles in action: The fieldbook for making connections, teaching, and the human brain.* Victoria, Australia: Hawker Brownlow.

Catterall, J., Chapleau, R., & Iwanga, J. (1999, Fall). *Involvement in the arts and human development: Extending an analysis of general associations and introducing the special cases of intense involvement in music and in theater arts* (Monograph Series No. 11). Washington, DC: Americas for the Arts.

Checkley, K. (1999). *Math in the early grades: Laying a foundation for later learning.* Alexandria, VA: Association for Supervision and Curriculum Development.

Chung, S.-C., Tack, G. –R., Choi, M.–H., Lee, S.–J, Choi, J.-S., Yi, J.-H, Park, S.-J. (2009). Changes in reaction time when using oxygen inhalation during simple visual matching tasks. *Neuroscience Letters, 453*(3), 173–177.

Coggins, D., Kravin, D., Coates, G. D., & Carrol, M. D. (2007). *English language learners in the mathematics classroom.* Thousand Oaks, CA: Corwin.

Collier, C. (2010). *RTI for diverse learners: More than 200 instructional interventions.* Thousand Oaks, CA: Corwin.

The Consortium: The Conference Board, Corporate Voices for Working Families, Partnership for 21st Century Skills, Society for Human Resource Management. (2006). *Are they really ready to work? Employers' perspectives on the basic knowledge and applied skills of new entrants to the 21st century workforce.* Washington, DC: Author.

Cooper, N., & Garner, B. K. (2012). *Developing a learning classroom: Moving beyond management through relationships, relevance, and rigor.* Thousand Oaks, CA: Corwin.

Costa, A. L. (1991). *Teaching for intelligent behavior: Outstanding strategies for strengthening your students' thinking skills.* Bellevue, WA: Bureau of Education and Research.

Costa, A. L. (2008). *The school as a home for the mind: Creating mindful curriculum, instruction, and dialogue* (2nd ed.). Victoria, Australia: Hawker Brownlow Education.

Covey, S. (1996). *The seven habits of highly effective people.* Salt Lake City, UT: Covey Leadership Center.

Covili, J. (2012). *Going Google: Powerful tools for the 21st century.* Thousand Oaks, CA: Corwin.

Curtain-Phillips, M. (2008). *How to make the most of math manipulatives—A fresh look at getting students' heads and hands around math concepts.* Retrieved August 31, 2009, from http://www.mathgoodies.com/articles/ manipulatives.html.

Davis, L. (2002). *The importance of field trips.* Retrieved August 21, 2009, from http: //gsa.confex.com.gsa/2002RM/finalprogram/abstract_33868.htr

Dean, C. B., Hubbell, E. R., Pitler, H., & Stone, B. J. (2012). *Classroom instruction that works: Research-based strategies for increasing student achievement,* 2nd ed. Alexandria, VA: Association for Supervision and Curriculum Development.

Delandtsheer, J. (2011). *Making all kids smarter: Strategies that help all students reach their highest potential.* Thousand Oaks, CA: Corwin.

Dewar, G. (2008–2014). *The cognitive benefits of play: Effects on the learning brain.* Retrieved March 5, 2015, from www.parentingscience.com/benefits-of-pl

Dewey, J. (1934). *Art as experience.* New York: Minion Ballet.

Dewey, J. (1938). *Experience and education.* New York: Macmillan.

Drake, S. (1996). Guided imagery and education. Theory, practice, and experience. *Journal of Mental Imagery, 20,* 1–58.

Ekwall, E. E., & Shanker, J. L. (1988). *Diagnosis and remediation of the disabled reader* (3rd ed.). Boston: Allyn and Bacon.

Feinstein, S. G. (2004). *Secrets of the teenage brain: Research-based strategies for reaching and teaching today's adolescents.* Thousand Oaks, CA: Corwin.

Feinstein, S. G. (2009). *Secrets of the teenage brain: Research-based strategies for reaching and teaching today's adolescents* (2nd ed.). Thousand Oaks, CA: Corwin.

Fisher, M. (2013). *Digital learning strategies.* Alexandria, VA: Association for Supervision and Curriculum Development.

Fogarty, R. (2009). *Brain-compatible classrooms* (3rd ed.). Victoria, Australia: Hawker Brownlow.

Fraser, L. (2013). *The benefits of drawing.* Retrieved March 4, 2015, www.the drawing-website.com/…/the-bene

Frontline. (2010, February 2). *Digital native map.* Retrieved March 15, 2015, from http://www.pbs.org/wgbh/pages/frontline/digitalnation/extras/digital_native.html Arlington, VA: Public Broadcasting Service.

Gardner, H. (1983). *Frames of mind: The theory of multiple intelligences.* New York: Basic Books.

Garner, R. (2005). *Humor, analogy, and metaphor: H.A.M. it up in teaching.* Retrieved March 5, 2015, from www.radicalpedagogy.org/…/Humor,_A

George, E. M., & Coch, D. (2011). Music training and working memory: An ERP study. *Neuropsychologia, 49,* 1083–1094.

Glasser, W. (1999). *Choice theory: A new psychology of personal freedom.* New York: HarperCollins.

Glynn, S. (1996). Teaching with analogies: Building on the science textbook. *The Reading Teacher, 49,* 490–492.

Graham, S., & Perin, D. (2007). A meta-analysis of writing instruction for adolescent students. *Journal of Educational Psychology, 99*(3), 445–476.

Green, L. S., & Casale-Giannola, D. (2011). *40 active learning strategies for the block schedule.* Thousand Oaks, CA: Corwin.

Greene, J., & Kisida, B. (2013). *Research: School field trips give significant benefits.* Retrieved March 5, 2015, from www.news.uark.edu/…/research-school-field.

Gregory, G. H., & Chapman, C. (2013). *Differentiated instructional strategies: One size doesn't fit all.* Thousand Oaks, CA: Corwin.

Gregory, G. H., & Herndon, L. E. (2010). *Differentiated instructional strategies for the block schedule.* Thousand Oaks, CA: Corwin.

Gregory, G. H., & Parry, T. (2006). *Designing brain-compatible learning* (3rd ed.). Thousand Oaks, CA: Corwin.

Hattie, J. (2009). *Visible learning: A synthesis of over 800 meta-analyses relating to achievement.* London: Routledge.

Institute for the Advancement of Research in Education (IARE). (2003). *Graphic organizers: A review of scientifically based research.* Portland, OR: Author.

Jensen, E. (1995). *Brain-based learning & teaching.* Del Mar, CA: The Brain Store.

Jensen, E. (2000). Moving with the brain in mind. *Educational Leadership, 58*(3), 34–37.

Jensen, E. (2001). *Arts with the brain in mind.* Alexandria, VA: Association for Supervision and Curriculum Development.

Jensen, E. (2005). *Top tunes for teaching: 977 song titles and practical tools for choosing the right music every time.* Thousand Oaks, CA: Corwin.

Jensen, E. (2007). *Brain-compatible strategies* (2nd ed.). Victoria, Australia: Hawker Brownlow Education.

Jensen, E. (2008). *Brain-based learning: The new paradigm of teaching.* Thousand Oaks, CA: Corwin.

Jensen, E. (2009a). *Fierce teaching: Purpose, passion, and what matters most.* Thousand Oaks, CA: Corwin.

Jensen, E. (2009b). *Super teaching* (4th ed.). Thousand Oaks, CA: Corwin.

Jensen, E., & Nickelsen, L. (2008). *Deeper learning: 7 powerful strategies for in-depth and longer-lasting learning.* Victoria, Australia: Hawker Brownlow.

Johnson, D. W., Johnson, R. T., & Holubec, E. J. (1994). *The new circles of learning: Cooperation in the classroom and school.* Alexandria, VA: Association for Supervision and Curriculum Development.

Jones, C. (2008). *The magic of metaphor.* Retrieved August 10, 2009, from http://www.Uxmatters.com/mt/archives/2008/php

Karten, T. J. (2008). *More inclusion strategies that work!* Victoria, Australia: Hawker Brownlow Education.

Karten, T. J. (2009). *Inclusion strategies that work for adolescent learners.* Thousand Oaks, CA: Corwin.

Kelly, M. (2014, June 25). *Neural sweet talk: Taste metaphors emotionally engage the brain.* Retrieved March 5, 2015, from www.princeton.edu>...>News>Archive

Kim, A. H., Vaugh, S., Wanzek, J., & Wei, S. (2004). Graphic organizers and their effects on the reading comprehension of students with LD: A synthesis of research. *Journal of Learning Disabilities, 37*(2), 105–118.

Krepel, W. J., & Duvall, C. R. (1981). *Field trips: A guide for planning and conducting educational experiences.* Washington, DC: National Education Association.

Kuhlmann, S., Kirschbaum, C., & Wolf, O. T. (2005, March). Effects of oral cortisol treatment in healthy young women on memory retrieval of negative and neutral words. *Neurobiology of Learning and Memory, 83,* 158–162.

Longcamp, M., Boucard, C., Gilhodes, J. C., Anton, J. L., Roth, M., Nazarian, B., & Velay, J. L. (2008). Learning through hand- or typewriting influences visual recognition of new graphic shapes: Behavioral and functional imaging evidence, *Journal of Cognitive Neuroscience, 20*(5), 802–815.

Mahoney, S. (2005, July/August). How to live longer. *American Association of Retired People, 48*(4B), 64–72.

Markowitz, K., & Jensen, E. (2007). *The great memory book.* Heatherton, Victoria, Australia: Hawker Brownlow Education.

Marsh, R. (2013). *Effects of storytelling in education: Imagery arts—foundation of intelligence and knowledge.* Retrieved February 25, 2015, from http://www.Richardmarsh.ie/effects.htm

Marzano, R. J. (2007). *The art and science of teaching.* Alexandria, VA: Association for Supervision and Curriculum Development.

McLaughlin, M., & Overturf, B. J. (2013). *The common core: Teaching K–5 students to meet the reading standards.* Newark, DE: International Reading Association.

Melber, L. M., & Hunter, A. (2010). *Integrating language arts and social studies: 25 strategies for K–8 inquiry-based learning.* Thousand Oaks, CA: Sage.

Nash, R. (2012). *From seatwork to feetwork: Engaging students in their own learning.* Thousand Oaks, CA: Corwin.

National Council for the Social Studies. (2010). *National curriculum standards for social studies: A framework for teaching, learning, and assessment.* Silver Springs, MD: National Council for the Social Studies.

National Council of Teachers of Mathematics (Eds.). (2000). *Principles and standards for school mathematics.* Reston, VA: Author.

National Governors Association Center for Best Practices, Council of Chief State School Officers. (2010). Common Core State Standards for English Language Arts & Literacy in History/Social Studies, Science, and Technical Subjects: Appendix B: Text Exemplars and Sample Performance Tasks. Washington, DC: Author.

National Science Teachers Association (NSTA). (2006). Picturing to learn makes science visual. *NSTA Reports, 18*(2), 20.

Palincsar, A. S., & Brown, A. L. (1984). Reciprocal teaching in comprehension-fostering and comprehension-monitoring activities. *Cognition and Instruction, 1*(2), 117–175.

Park, M.-H., Park, E.-J., Choi, J., Chai, S., Lee, J.-H., Lee, C., et al. (2011, December). Preliminary study of Internet addiction and cognitive function in adolescents based on IQ tests. *Psychiatry Research, 190,* 275–281.

PBS. (2014, September 3). *Arts & the mind.* Retrieved March 4, 2015, from www.pbs. org/program/arts-mind/

Perez, K. (2008). *More than 100 brain-friendly tools and strategies for literacy instruction.* Thousand Oaks, CA: Corwin.

Popova, M. (2015, February 8). *The magic of metaphor: What children's minds reveal about the evolution of the imagination.* Retrieved March 5, 2015, from https://twitter.com/.../570760923763351

Posamentier, A. S., & Hauptman, H. A. (2006). *101+ great ideas for introducing key concepts in mathematics: A resource for secondary school teachers* (2nd ed.). Thousand Oaks, CA: Corwin.

Posamentier, A. S., & Jaye, D. (2006). *What successful math teachers do, Grades 6–12: 79 research-based strategies for the standards-based classroom.* Thousand Oaks, CA: Corwin.

Prensky, M. (2006). *Don't bother me, Mom—I'm learning!* St. Paul, MN: Paragon House.

Prensky, M. (2009, February). H. Sapiens Digital: From digital immigrants and digital natives to digital wisdom. *Innovate: Journal of Online Education, 5*(3).

Prystay, C. (2004, December 13). As math skills slip, U.S. schools seek answers from Asia. *The Wall Street Journal,* pp. A1–A8.

Ronis, D. L. (2006). *Brain-compatible mathematics* (2nd ed.). Thousand Oaks, CA: Corwin.

Rothstein, A. S., Rothstein, E., & Lauber, G. (2006). *Write for mathematics* (2nd ed.). Thousand Oaks, CA: Corwin.

Scott, D., & Marzano, R. J. (2014). *Awaken the learner: Finding the source of effective education.* Bloomington, IN: Marzano Research Laboratory.

Sebesta, L. M., & Martin, S. R. M. (2004). Fractions: Building a foundation with concrete manipulatives. *Illinois Schools Journal, 83*(2), 3–23.

Secretary's Commission on Achieving Necessary Skills (SCANS). (1991). *What work requires of schools: A SCANS report for America 2000.* Washington, DC: U.S. Department of Labor.

Sousa, D. A. (2006). *How the brain learns* (3rd ed.). Thousand Oaks, CA: Corwin.

Sousa, D. A. (2007). *How the special needs brain learns* (2nd ed.). Thousand Oaks, CA: Corwin.

Sousa, D. A. (2011). *How the brain learns* (4th ed.). Thousand Oaks, CA: Corwin.

Sousa, D. A. (2012). *Brainwork: The neuroscience behind how we lead others.* Bloomington, IN: Triple Nickel Press.

Sousa, D. A., & Pilecki, T. (2013). *From STEM to STEAM: Using brain-compatible strategies to integrate the arts.* Thousand Oaks, CA: Corwin.

Sousa, D., & Tomlinson, C. (2011). *Differentiation and the brain: How neuro-science supports the learner-friendly classroom.* Bloomington, IN: Solution Tree Press.

Sprenger, M. (2007a). *Becoming a "wiz" at brain-based teaching: How to make every year your best year* (2nd ed.). Thousand Oaks, CA: Corwin.

Sprenger, M. (2007b). *Memory 101 for educators.* Thousand Oaks, CA: Corwin.

Sprenger, M. (2008). *The developing brain: Birth to age eight.* Thousand Oaks, CA: Corwin.

Sprenger, M. (2010). *Brain-based teaching in the digital age.* Alexandria, VA: Association for Supervision and Curriculum Development.

Stauffer, R. G. (1975). *Directing the direct reading-thinking process.* New York: Harper & Row.

Sternberg, R. J., & Grigorenko, E. L. (2000). *Teaching for successful intelligence: To increase student learning and achievement.* Arlington Heights, IL: Skylight.

Stibich, M. (2014, May 1). Retrieved February 25, 2015, from longevity.about.com >About Health.

Strong, R. W., Silver, H. F., Perini, M. J., & Tuculescu, G. M. (2002). *Reading for academic success: Powerful strategies for struggling, average, and advanced readers, grades 7–12.* Thousand Oaks, CA: Corwin.

Summey, D. C. (2013). *Developing digital literacies: A framework for professional learning.* Thousand Oaks, CA: Corwin.

Tate, M. L. (2009). *Mathematics worksheets don't grow dendrites: 20 numeracy strategies that engage the brain.* Thousand Oaks, CA: Corwin.

Tate, M. L. (2012). *Social studies worksheets don't grow dendrites: 20 instructional strategies that engage the brain.* Thousand Oaks, CA: Corwin.

Tate, M. L. (2014a). *Reading and language arts worksheets don't grow dendrites: 20 literacy strategies that engage the brain.* Thousand Oaks, CA: Corwin.

Tate, M. L. (2014b). *Shouting won't grow dendrites: 20 techniques to detour around the danger zones* (2nd ed.). Thousand Oaks, CA: Corwin.

Tate, M. L., & Phillips, W. G. (2011). *Science worksheets don't grow dendrites: 20 instructional strategies that engage the brain.* Thousand Oaks, CA: Corwin.

Tileston, D. W. (2011). *Closing the RTI gap: Why poverty and culture count.* Bloomington, IN: Solution Tree Press.

Tileston, D. W., & Darling, S. K. (2009). *Why culture counts: Teaching children of poverty.* Bloomington, IN: Solution Tree Press.

Todd, L. (2014). *How much learning happens on field trips? A lot, a new study says.* Retrieved March 20, 2015, from http://www.seattletimes.com/education-lab/how-much-learning-happens-on-field-trips-a-lot-a-new-study-says/

Udvari-Solner, A., & Kluth, P. (2008). *Joyful learning: Active and collaborative learning in inclusive classrooms.* Thousand Oaks, CA: Corwin.

University of Arkansas. (2014, October 16). *Major benefits for students who attend live theater.* Retrieved March 5, 2015, www.sciencedaily.com/.../141016165953

Wall, E. S., & Posamentier, A. S. (2006). *What successful math teachers do, Grades PreK–5: 47 research-based strategies for the standards-based classroom.* Thousand Oaks, CA: Corwin.

Walsh, J., & Sattes, B. (2005). *Quality questioning: Research-based practice to engage every learner.* Thousand Oaks, CA: Corwin.

Widrich, L. (2012). *The science of storytelling: What listening to a story does to our brains.* Retrieved February 25, 2015, from blog.bufferapp.com/science-of-storytelling-why.

Wiggins, G., & McTighe, J. (2008, May). Put understanding first. *Educational Leadership, 65*(19), 36–41.

Wiley-Blackwell, (2009, February 11). Adolescents involved with music do better in school. *ScienceDaily.* Retrieved January 7, 2015, from www.sciencedaily.com/releases/2009/02/090210110043.htm

Willis, J. (2006). *Research-based strategies to ignite student learning.* Alexandria, VA: Association for Supervision and Curriculum Development.

Willis, J. (2007a). *Brain-friendly strategies for the inclusion classroom.* Alexandria, VA: Association for Supervision and Curriculum Development.

Willis, J. (2007b, Summer). *The neuroscience of joyful education.* Retrieved July 20, 2007, from www.ascd.org.80

Wolfe, P., & Nevills, P. (2004). *Building the reading brain. PreK–3.* Thousand Oaks, CA: Corwin.

Wonacott, M. E. (1993). *Apprenticeship and the future of the workplace.* Retrieved September 3, 2009, from http://www.ericdigests.org/1992-3/future.htm

Zhou, Y., Lin, F.-C., Du, Y.-S., Qin, L.-D., Zhao, Z.-M., Xu, J.-R., et al. (2011, July). Gray matter abnormalities in Internet addiction: A voxel-based morphometry study. *European Journal of Radiology, 79,* 92–95.

# Index

Acronyms, 89. *See also* Mnemonic devices
Acrostics, 89. *See also* Mnemonic devices
Affirmations, 68
Allen, Rich, 111
Alphabet book, 189
Analogies. *See* Metaphors, analogies, and
    similes
*Antigone*, 1–3, 194, 195, 198, 199
Appointment clock, 99, 99 (figure)
Appointment timeline, 100 (figure)
Apprenticeships. *See* Work study
    and apprenticeships
Aristotle, 4, 34
Artists' greatest hits, 112
Artwork. *See* Drawing and artwork
Assessment, 194–195
Attention
    paying, 131 (figure)
    ways to gain/maintain, 195–198
Auditory learning modality. *See* Learning
    modalities
Autry Technology Center, 177

Bingo, 44
Bloom's taxonomy, 20 (figure)
Board games, 39, 41
Body spell, 139
Brain-compatible instruction, 4–12
    characteristics of environment, 8–12
    compared to multiple intelligences and
        learning theory, 12–13 (figure)
Brain-compatible lesson plan, 193–200
    assessment, 194–195
    blank template, 201
    content chunks, 198–199
    content delivery strategies, 199–200
    lesson objectives, 193–194
    sample lessons, 202–204
    ways to gain/maintain attention,
        195–198
Brain-derived neurotrophic
    factor (BDNF), 98
Brainstorming and discussion, 15–22
    Bloom's taxonomy and, 20 (figure)
    defining the strategy, 15

instructional activities, 17–21
reflection and application, 22
theoretical framework, 16

Can and can't, 163
Candy Land, 41
Caracas, Gloria, 147
Career day, 179
Carrey, Jim, 66
Cartoons, 68
Cause and effect, 148
Cause/effect organizer, 55 (figure),
    212 (figure)
Challenge, 11
*Challenger* space shuttle, 198
Character traits, 51 (figure),
    206 (figure)
Charades, 42. *See also* Role plays, drama,
    pantomimes, and charades
Chinese proverb, 4, 169
Chunking, 11–12, 198–199
Cinquain, 113
Circumference conga, 102
Class clown, 66
Classical music, 111
Clocks, 99, 99 (figure)
Close reading, 17
Colonies story, 147
Common Core State Standards, 194
Compare/contrast organizer, 57 (figure),
    218 (figure)
Comparison organizer, 55 (figure),
    213 (figure)
Competencies, 179
"Conga" (Estefan), 102
Content
    chunking, 11–12, 198–199
    smarter teaching, 199–200
    students talking and moving, 10
Continent story, 145
Controversial issues, 21
Cooperative learning.
        *See* Reciprocal teaching and
        cooperative learning
Cycle organizer, 56 (figure), 214 (figure)

Dendrite growers, 6, 7, 59 (figure)
Digital differentiation, 156
Digital storytelling, 157
Directed Reading Thinking Activity
    (DR-TA), 17
Disc jockey, 109
Discussion. *See* Brainstorming and
    discussion
Document camera, 155–156
DOVE guidelines, 17
Drama. *See* Role plays, drama,
    pantomimes, and charades
Drawing and artwork, 25–30
    defining the strategy, 25
    instructional activities, 26–29
    reflection and application, 30
    theoretical framework, 26
Drill partner, 132

Emotion, 197–198
Endorphins, 64
*Engage the Brain: Graphic Organizers and
    Other Visual Strategies*, 59
Engage the Brain Games, 46
Estefan, Gloria, 102
Estes, Eleanor, 49
Ethnography, 36
Events sequences 45, 109
*Everything I Needed to Know I Learned
    in Kindergarten*, 7
Expectations, 11
Experiments. *See* Manipulatives,
    experiments, labs, and models

Families, in class, 19, 130
Feedback, positive, 68
Field trips, 33–37
    defining the strategy, 33
    instructional activities, 34–36
    reflection and application, 37
    theoretical framework, 34
Figurative language, 148
5Ws and an H, 54, 54 (figure), 211 (figure)
Foundational skills, 179
Four square writing, 187
Fractions, 75

Games, 39–47
    defining the strategy, 39
    instructional activities, 41–46
    reflection and application, 47
    theoretical framework, 40
Garden, 36
Gardeners, 6
Gardner, Howard, 6, 73
Geometry, 43–44, 93, 140–141
Graphic organizers, semantic maps, and
    word webs, 49–60
    blank templates, 206–219
    defining the strategy, 49

instructional activities, 51–59
reflection and application, 60
theoretical framework, 50
Guided imagery. *See* Visualization and
    guided imagery

Habits of mind, 64
*Have You Read Any Math Lately?*, 148
High-stakes testing, 4
Hippocampus, 196
History
    field trips, 35
    games, 44
Humor, 63–70
    defining the strategy, 63
    instructional activities, 64–69
    reflection and application, 70
    theoretical framework, 64
*Hundred Dresses, The* (Estes), 49
Hunter, Madeline, 194, 198, 199
*Hustle, The* (McCoy), 102

Imagery. *See* Visualization and
    guided imagery
Imagination, 165
*I'm as Quick as a Cricket* (Wood), 83
Instructional activities
    brainstorming and discussion, 17–21
    drawing and artwork, 26–29
    field trips, 34–36
    games, 41–46
    graphic organizers, semantic maps, and
        word webs, 51–59
    humor, 64–69
    manipulatives, experiments, labs, and
        models, 74–77
    metaphors, analogies, and similes,
        83–85
    mnemonic devices, 90–93
    movement, 99–103
    music, rhythm, rhyme, and rap,
        109–113
    project-based and problem-based
        instruction, 119–123
    reciprocal teaching and cooperative
        learning, 129–133
    role plays, drama, pantomimes, and
        charades, 138–141
    storytelling, 146–150
    technology, 155–158
    visualization and guided imagery,
        163–165
    visuals, 171–173
    work study and apprenticeships,
        179–181
    writing and journals, 187–190
Internships. *See* Work study and
    apprenticeships
Interpersonal skills. *See* Social skills/
    interaction

Jazz music, 111
Jensen, Eric, 111
*Jeopardy,* 40, 42, 46
Jigsaw activity, 132–133
Jokes, 63, 65, 66
Journals. *See* Writing and journals

Kinesthetic learning modality.
    *See* Learning modalities
K-N-L graphic organizers, 51, 52 (figure),
    207 (figure)

Labs. *See* Manipulatives, experiments,
    labs, and models
Language arts
  games, 44
  manipulatives, experiments, labs,
      and models, 76
  metaphors, analogies, and similes, 83, 84
  mnemonic devices, 92
  movement activities, 101
  role plays, drama, pantomimes, and
      charades, 140, 141
  storytelling, 148
  writing and journals, 188
Laughing clubs, 63, 65
Learning modalities, 6, 12–13 (figure), 199
Lecturettes, 172, 187
Lesson objectives, 193–194
Lessons, relevant, 9
Logarithms, 84
Loop game, 43

Main idea with supporting details
    (table with legs), 53, 54 (figure),
    81, 210 (figure)
Manipulatives, experiments, labs, and
    models, 73–78
  defining the strategy, 73–74
  instructional activities, 74–77
  reflection and application, 78
  theoretical framework, 74
Maps. *See* Graphic organizers, semantic
    maps, and word webs; Story map
MATH acronym, 91
*Math and Children's Literature,* 149
*Math Curse* (Scieszka), 148
Mathematics
  drawing and artwork in, 27, 28, 29
  field trips, 35, 36
  games, 41, 42
  humor, 67
  manipulatives, experiments, labs, and
      models, 75
  metaphors, analogies, and
      similes, 83
  mnemonic devices, 91, 92, 93
  movement activities, 100, 101, 102
  project-based and problem-based
      instruction, 119, 120, 122

  role plays, drama, pantomimes, and
      charades, 139, 140
  storytelling, 148, 149
  visualization and guided imagery in,
      163, 164
  visuals, 172
  work study and apprenticeships, 180, 181
  writing and journals, 188
*Mathematics and Humor* (NCTM), 67
*Mathematics Worksheets Don't Grow
    Dendrites: 20 Numeracy Strategies That
    Engage the Brain PreK-8,* 7, 148
McAuliffe, Christa, 198
McCoy, Van, 102
Meaning, 82, 197
Media multitask, 154
Medicine, and visualization, 161–162
Memory pathways, 156
Metaphors, analogies, and similes, 81–86
  defining the strategy, 81–82
  instructional activities, 83–85
  reflection and application, 86
  theoretical framework, 82
Mind map, 58, 58 (figure), 219 (figure)
Mnemonic devices, 89–94
  defining the strategy, 89
  instructional activities, 90–93
  reflection and application, 94
  theoretical framework, 90
Models. *See* Manipulatives, experiments,
    labs, and models
Momentum shift, 11, 165
Moore, Connie, 91
Movement, 97–104
  defining the strategy, 97
  instructional activities, 99–103
  reflection and application, 104
  theoretical framework, 98
Multiple intelligences, 6, 12–13 (figure)
Muscle memory, 97
Museums, 35
Music
  in brain-compatible environment, 9
  drawing and artwork in, 28
  games, 46
  manipulatives, experiments, labs, and
      models, 73
  metaphors, analogies, and similes, 84
  movement activities, 101, 102
  reciprocal teaching and cooperatie
      learning, 133
  technology and, 158
Music, rhythm, rhyme, and rap strategy,
    107–114
  defining the strategy, 107–108
  instructional activities, 109–113
  reflection and application, 114
  theoretical framework, 108–109
My Stuff, Your Stuff, 129
My Turn, Your Turn, 129

Narrative chaining, 149
Need, student's, 196
New age music, 111
Nonlinguistic representation, 50
Note-taking, 157, 185
Novelty, 196–197
Number line hustle, 102–103

Objectives, lesson, 193–197
Organizers. *See* Graphic organizers,
    semantic maps, and word webs
Outside classes, 35

Pantomimes. *See* Role plays, drama,
    pantomimes, and charades
Partner reading, 132
*Password*, 45, 46
Pearl Harbor, 33
Peer-to-peer tutoring, 128
People Search, 43
Phillips, Warren, 76, 110, 147, 181
Physical education, 39, 165
Piano music, 111
Pictionary, 27, 46
PIE (persuade, inform, express,
    entertain), 188
Planetarium, 35
Point of view, 148
Positive energy stick, 68
Positive environment, 8
Positive feedback, 68
PowerPoint, 157, 171
Practicums. *See* Work study and
    apprenticeships
*Price Is Right, The*, 46, 97, 102
Problem/solution organizer, 57 (figure),
    217 (figure)
Procedural memory, 97, 98, 156
Process observer, 131, 132
Project-based and problem-based
    instruction, 117–124
    defining the strategy, 117–118
    instructional activities, 119–123
    reflection and application, 124
    theoretical framework, 118–119
Promethean board, 155
*Pygmalion in the Classroom*, 11

Questions, 18
    5Ws and an H, 54, 54 (figure),
        211 (figure)
Quick Writes, 189

Rap. *See* Music, rhythm, rhyme,
    and rap strategy
*Reader's Theater*, 140
Reading, partner, 132
*Reading and Language Arts Worksheets Don't
    Grow Dendrites: 20 Literacy Strategies
    That Engage the Brain*, 7

Recess, 39
Reciprocal teaching and cooperative
    learning, 127–134
    defining the strategy, 127–128
    instructional activities, 129–133
    reflection and application, 134
    theoretical framework, 128–129
Reflection and application
    brainstorming and discussions, 22
    drawing and artwork, 30
    field trips, 37
    games, 47
    graphic organizers, semantic maps, and
        word webs, 60
    humor, 70
    manipulatives, experiments, labs, and
        models, 78
    metaphors, analogies, and similes, 86
    mnemonic devices, 94
    movement, 104
    music, rhythm, rhyme, and rap, 114
    project-based and problem-based
        instruction, 124
    reciprocal teaching and cooperative
        learning, 134
    role plays, drama, pantomimes, and
        charades, 142
    storytelling, 151
    technology, 159
    visualization and guided imagery, 166
    visuals, 174
    work study and apprenticeships, 182
    writing and journals, 191
Rhyme. *See* Music, rhythm, rhyme, and
    rap strategy
Rhythm. *See* Music, rhythm, rhyme, and
    rap strategy
Richter Scale, 84
Riddle box, 67
Riddles, 66
Rituals, 10
Rock 'N Learn, 110
Role plays, drama, pantomimes, and
    charades, 137–142
    defining the strategy, 137
    games, 42
    instructional activities, 138–141
    reflection and application, 142
    theoretical framework, 138
Rosenthal, Robert, 11

SCANS Report, 154, 179
Scavenger hunt, 35
School-to-Work Opportunities
    Act (1994), 181
Science
    drawing and artwork in, 27, 28
    field trips, 35
    manipulatives, experiments, labs, and
        models, 76

mnemonic devices, 91, 93
project-based and problem-based
    instruction, 121
role plays, drama, pantomimes, and
    charades, 140
visualization and guided
    imagery in, 164
*Science Worksheets Don't Grow Dendrites: 20*
    *Instructional Strategies That Engage the*
    *Brain,* 7, 181
Seasonal appointment clock, 99, 99 (figure)
Semantic maps. *See* Graphic organizers,
    semantic maps, and word webs
Sentence starters, 20
Sequence of events, 148
Sequence organizer, 56 (figure),
    215 (figure)
Service-learning project, 180
Seven, series of, 11–12, 198–199
*Seven Habits of Highly Effective People,*
    *The,* 198
*Shouting Won't Grow Dendrites: 20*
    *Techniques to Detour Around*
    *the Danger Zones,* 7, 10, 69
*Sign Along Science* (Phillips), 110
Similes. *See* Metaphors, analogies,
    and similes
Singapore students, 26, 39, 163, 170
*Sir Cumference* (Neuschwander), 148
*"Sit & Get" Won't Grow Dendrites: 20*
    *Professional Learning Strategies That*
    *Engage the Adult Brain,* 7
SMART board, 155
Smarter teaching, 200
SMILE mnemonic, 8, 65
*Snake, The,* 97
Social skills/interaction, 107, 131, 154
Social studies
    drawing and artwork in, 27, 28
    field trips, 36
    metaphors, analogies, and similes, 85
    role plays, drama, pantomimes, and
        charades, 139, 140, 141
    visualization and guided imagery, 165
    visuals, 173
*Social Studies Worksheets Don't Grow*
    *Dendrites: 20 Instructional Strategies*
    *That Engage the Brain,* 7
Socrates, 34
Solar system, 35
SOLO pyramid, 18, 21 (figure)
*Songify,* 110
Sort and Report, 77
Speech, parts of, 149
Sponge activity, 120
Sports, and visualization, 161
Sticky notes, 76
Story maps, 52, 53 (figure), 209 (figure)
*Story of the Algebraic Equation, The,* 149–150
Story stool, 146–147

Storytelling, 145–151
    defining the strategy, 145
    digital, 157
    instructional activities, 146–150
    reflection and application, 151
    theoretical framework, 146
Strategies, 5–6
    brainstorming and discussion, 15
    drawing and artwork, 25
    field trips, 33
    games, 39
    graphic organizers, semantic maps,
        and word webs, 49
    humor, 63
    manipulatives, experiments, labs, and
        models, 73–74
    metaphors, analogies, and similes, 81–82
    mnemonic devices, 89
    movement, 97
    music, rhythm, rhyme, and rap, 107–108
    project-based and problem-based
        instruction, 117–118
    reciprocal teaching and cooperative
        learning, 127–128
    role plays, drama, pantomimes, and
        charades, 137
    storytelling, 145
    technology, 153
    visualization and guided imagery, 161
    visuals, 169
    work study and apprenticeships, 177
    writing and journals, 185
Stress, 11
Survey technique SQ3R, 171
SWITCH game, 41
Synthesis, 113

Table with legs, 53, 54 (figure),
    81, 210 (figure)
Tactile learning modality. *See* Learning
    modalities
Talent show, 113
Taxonomy, Bloom's, 20 (figure)
T-charts, 131
Technology, 153–159
    defining the strategy, 153
    instructional activities,
        155–158
    reflection and application, 159
    theoretical framework, 154–155
TEGO, 110
Tessellations, 29
Theoretical framework, 40
    brainstorming and discussions, 16
    drawing and artwork, 26
    field trips, 34
    games, 47
    graphic organizers, semantic maps, and
        word webs, 50
    humor, 64

manipulatives, experiments, labs, and models, 74
metaphors, analogies, and similes, 82
mnemonic devices, 90
movement, 98
music, rhythm, rhyme, and rap, 108–109
project-based and problem-based instruction, 118–119
reciprocal teaching and cooperative learning, 128–129
role plays, drama, pantomimes, and charades, 138
storytelling, 146
technology, 154–155
visualization and guided imagery, 162–163
visuals, 170
work study and apprenticeships, 178
writing and journals, 186
Think, pair, share technique, 20, 132
Thinking proficiencies, 19
3-Ps (page, paragraph, passing), 132
Thumbs up/thumbs down, 76
Tired words, 188
Topic description organizer, 57 (figure), 216 (figure)
*Top Tunes for Teaching* (Jensen), 111
TWA (Teaching with Analogies), 83
Twitter, 81
Typing, 185

*Ultimate Book of Music for Learning, The* (Allen & Wood), 111
*U.S.S. Arizona* Memorial, 33

VAKT (visual, auditory, kinesthetic, tactile), 6, 12–13 (figure), 199
Venn diagrams, 85
Video games, 11
Virtual field trips, 36
Visualization and guided imagery, 161–166
defining the strategy, 161

instructional activities, 163–165
reflection and application, 166
theoretical framework, 162–163
Visual learning modality. *See* VAKT
Visuals, 169–174
in brain-compatible environment, 8–9
defining the strategy, 169
instructional activities, 171–173
reflection and application, 174
theoretical framework, 170
Visual-spatial intelligence, 73
Vocabulary words, 27, 41–42, 45, 75
Vocabulary word web, 52 (figure), 208 (figure)

*Wheel of Fortune,* 40, 43, 46
*When Charlie McButton Lost Power,* 81
Who Am I? game, 45
*Who Wants to Be a Millionaire?,* 45
Wood, Audrey, 83
Wood, W. W., 111
Word wall, 173
Word web, vocabulary, 52 (figure), 208 (figure)
Word webs. *See* Graphic organizers, semantic maps, and word webs
*Worksheets Don't Grow Dendrites: 20 Instructional Strategies That Engage the Brain,* 7
Work study and apprenticeships, 177–182
defining the strategy, 177
instructional activities, 179–181
reflection and application, 182
theoretical framework, 178
Writing and journals, 185–191
defining the strategy, 185
instructional activities, 187–190
reflection and application, 191
theoretical framework, 186
Writing process, 189

**CORWIN**

A SAGE Company

**CORWIN HAS ONE MISSION:** to enhance education through intentional professional learning.

We build long-term relationships with our authors, educators, clients, and associations who partner with us to develop and continuously improve the best evidence-based practices that establish and support lifelong learning.

# utions you want. Experts you trust. Results you need.

### AUTHOR CONSULTING

**Author Consulting**

On-site professional learning with sustainable results! Let us help you design a professional learning plan to meet the unique needs of your school or district.
www.corwin.com/pd

### INSTITUTES

**Institutes**

Corwin Institutes provide collaborative learning experiences that equip your team with tools and action plans ready for immediate implementation.
www.corwin.com/institutes

### ECOURSES

**eCourses**

Practical, flexible online professional learning designed to let you go at your own pace.
www.corwin.com/ecourses

### READ2EARN

**Read2Earn**

Did you know you can earn graduate credit for reading this book? Find out how:
www.corwin.com/read2earn

Contact an account manager at (800) 831-6640 or visit **www.corwin.com** for more information.